GWS

STEAM ECHOES

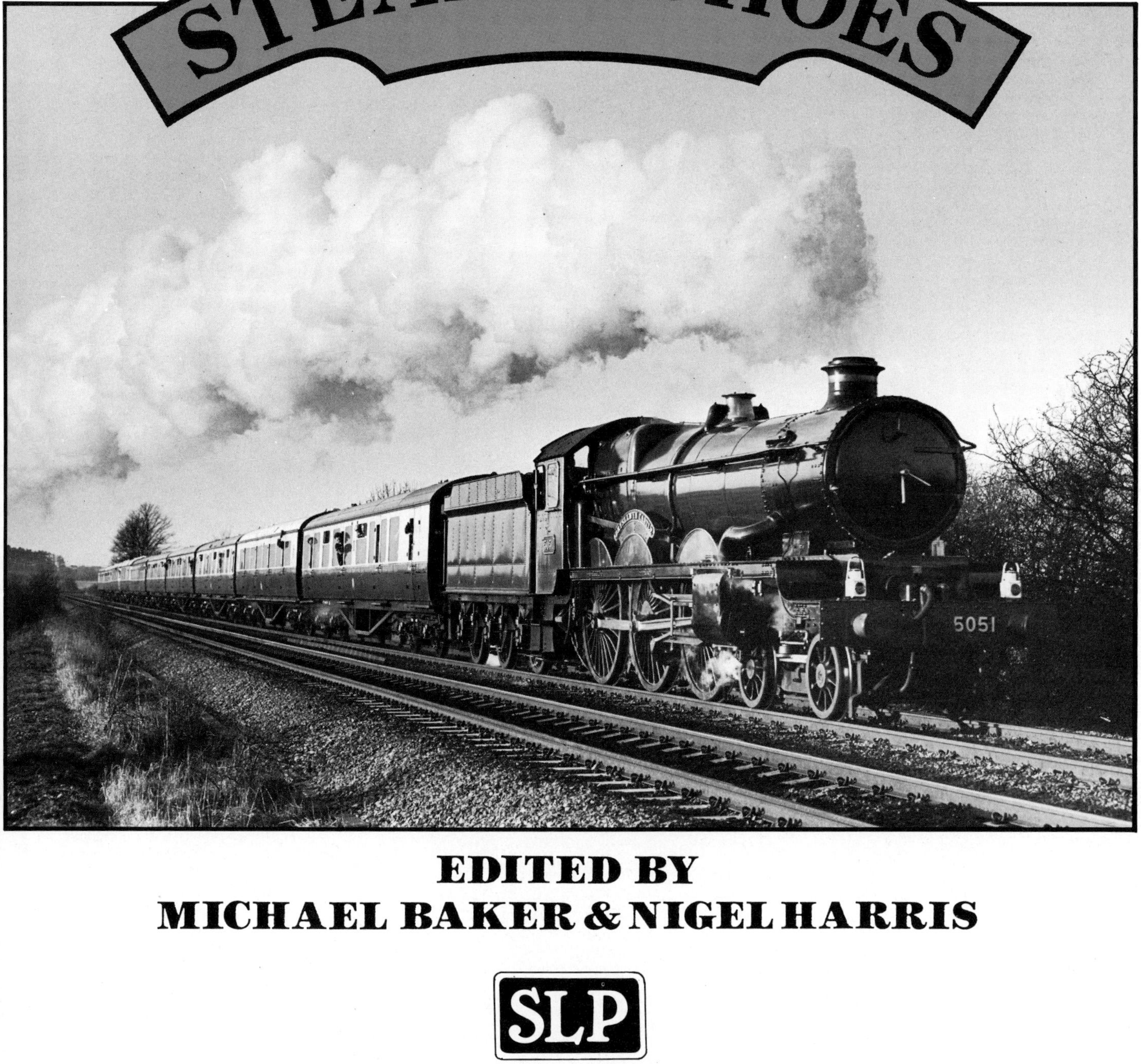

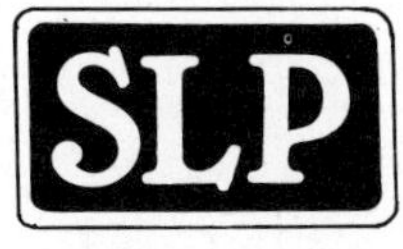

EDITED BY
MICHAEL BAKER & NIGEL HARRIS

SLP
Silver Link Publishing
5 HAWK ST, CARNFORTH, LANCASHIRE, LA5 9LA

Steam echoes: 25th anniversary of the Great
Western Society.
I. Baker, Michael, 1937- II. Harris, Nigel
625.2'61'06042579   TJ609.4.G7
ISBN 0–947971–06–8

Above: GWR 'Hall' 4–6–0 No. 5900 *Hinderton Hall*, in gleaming condition, stands in the shed yard at Didcot Railway Centre, with just a trace of steam above the cylinders to indicate that the locomotive is ready for work, September 29 1979. *Mark Wilkins*.

CONTENTS

Designed by Nigel Harris.
Front cover design by Phil Cousins.

Typeset by Dentset, Oxford.
Printed in the UK by Netherwood Dalton & Co. Ltd, Huddersfield, Yorkshire.

FRONT COVER: No. 5051 *Drysllwyn Castle* steams away from Stratford upon Avon on January 26 1980 with 'The Sunset' railtour — the last main line outing of the Great Western Society vintage train. *John Cooper-Smith*

INSIDE FRONT COVER: The Society's 14XX 0–4–2T No. 1466 tackles Tenterden bank, during its visit to the Kent & East Sussex Railway in 1984. *Alan Crotty*

PREVIOUS PAGE: The GWS on the main line. On January 26 1980, 'Castle' 4–6–0 No. 5051 *Drysllwyn Castle* forges up the bank out of Leamington, towards Harbury, with 'The Sunset' railtour. *R.J. Blenkinsop.*

LEFT: In September 1964, the sun sets behind Collett '14XX' 0–4–2T No. 1444, during a GWS auto-train railtour. *Angus Davis.*

INSIDE BACK COVER: Didcot Railway Centre, September 29 1984. *Mike Esau*

BACK COVER (TOP): On September 29 1979, '43XX' No. 5322 bathes in late evening sunshine at the Didcot Railway centre. *Mark Wilkins.*
LOWER: Nos 5900 *Hinderton Hall* and 6998 *Burton Agnes Hall* pass Leamington on railtour duty on May 15 1976. *R.J. Blenkinsop.*

FOREWORD
by
HIS GRACE
THE DUKE OF MARLBOROUGH

Blenheim Palace.

25th February, 1986

It gives me great pleasure as President of the Thames
& Chilterns Tourist Board, an organisation dedicated
to fostering the growth of the tourist industry in
Oxfordshire, to salute the achievements of the Great
Western Society. In twenty-five years it has become
one of the county's most important tourist attractions.

From an enthusiast's campaign to raise £1,130 to buy a
tank engine in 1961, which was not even going to be
kept in Oxfordshire, the Society has gone on to create
a fascinating range of GWR rolling stock and buildings
at Didcot which is one of the best of all collections
from the pre-nationalisation era. It is scarcely surpr-
rising then, that in 1985 when the GWR celebrations
were held at Didcot, 71,500 people went there on visits.

The enthusiasm and commitment of the Society's members
is remarkable as they continue to raise money and
harness Government grants for the restoration of steam
engines and further improvements to the Didcot site.
Although very much a team effort, the contribution of
Graham Perry, the Society's Chairman, deserves special
mention. He was one of those four people who set out
to buy the tank engine in 1961.

I am one of those "children of all ages" who finds steam
railways hugely fascinating. I have greatly enjoyed my
own visits to Didcot and I hope that you will too!

Marlborough

CHAPTER 1

THE EARLY YEARS OF THE
GREAT WESTERN SOCIETY
1961–1967

Frank Dumbleton

IMAGINE a sultry August afternoon. The black painted steelwork of the footbridge over the track is hot to touch. The atmosphere is heavy with steam locomotive odours — smoke, steam, oil and soot — with the addition to the cocktail of a uniquely Southall ingredient: the smell of roasted wheat being 'shot from guns' in the nearby 'Quaker Oats' factory.

The wooden floorboards of the footbridge have been charred over the years by cinders sent skywards from locomotive chimneys and gaps have been burned between many of the timbers. Now that the boards have been thoroughly dried by the summer sun, most of them have shrunk and loosened, tipping to and

fro as you walk on them. Anybody who ignores the threat of a forty shilling penalty, detailed on the GWR cast iron signs, and cycles across the footbridge, has his felony advertised to all and sundry by the rumbling and rattling of loose boards under the bicycle wheels.

The cyclist trundling towards us, heralded by a noise like the distant rumbling of summer thunderstorms, is Jon Barlow. This is the first time he has put in an appearance since coming back from holiday and he looks worried. He is clutching the current issue of the 'Railway Magazine' in which is printed, above his name and address, a letter inviting subscriptions towards the

Above: The footbridge from which this photograph was taken, at Southall, was the birthplace of the Great Western Society in 1961, when four schoolboy trainspotters decided to buy a Collett '14XX' 0–4–2T. Rattling through Southall in the evening of June 28 1960 is 'Hall' 4–6–0 No 6942 *Eshton Hall*, in charge of a down train of milk empties. Allocated to Old Oak Common (81A), this locomotive survived in service until December 1964 and was cut up for scrap by Cashmore's yard, Newport, in April 1965. Destruction of this kind spurred the GWS into very rapid development. *Mike Pope.*

preservation of a '14XX' (formerly '48XX') class auto-train locomotive.

"What are we going to do now?" he says. "I've got some replies at home and one person is offering a

Above: Collett 'Castle' 4–6–0 No. 5055 *Earl of Eldon* sprints through Southall on August 10 1957, heading for Paddington with a lengthy express. Note the water column, drain 'funnel' and cast-iron stove on the platform end: the GWS is as enthusiastic about the preservation of equipment such as this as it is about the altogether more glamorous locomotives and chocolate and cream liveried stock. *GWS Collection.*

Right: '57XX' 0–6–0PT No. 5755 comes off the Brentford branch with a lengthy train of empty wagons, in 1950. *C.R.L. Coles.*

£10 donation if we can convince him we're serious."

"How about a committee meeting?" suggests somebody helpfully. That was the August of 1961 and the organisation which was born then has been carried forward for the past 25 years on an unstoppable wave of enthusiasm for the Great Western Railway. The popular legend of the railway preservation movement is that the Great Western Society was formed by four Southall schoolboys, and this is essentially true. Jon Barlow lived in Hounslow and went to Isleworth Grammar School. His school mates there, Angus Davis and Mike Peart, lived in Southall and Heston respectively. Graham Perry lived in Southall and went to school in Hounslow. They all did their trainspotting on the footbridge spanning the WR main line from Paddington, at Southall.

When you are sixteen years old, as they were in 1961, the simple underlining of names and numbers in a book begins to take second place to a more detailed appreciation of what is going on around you, and the steam railway of Southall became theatre of the most dramatic kind. From the footbridge, just to the east of the station, you could survey express and local passenger trains, freight trains, inter-yard transfer workings and the comings and goings of the engine shed. The approach of a westbound express train could be watched for several minutes because, looking towards London, there were no bridges over

A classic GWR combination: '14XX' 0–4–2T No. 1458 and auto-trailer at Southall, May 3 1958. *R.C. Riley.*

the line to obscure the view for nearly three miles. At Southall, nine miles west of Paddington, the locomotive would still be working hard to gain speed with a heavy train.

An express train travelling east, towards London, was a different matter altogether, suddenly bursting through the road bridge at the far end of the platform and, a few seconds later, racing under the footbridge in a swirling cloud of steam and smoke. If you hurried after leaving school for the day you could arrive at the footbridge in time to see the Up 'Cornish Riviera Express' rush through Southall with its chocolate and cream carriages headed by a 'King' 4–6–0.

Many local trains were worked by diesel multiple units by this time, but some services were still headed by '61XX' class 2–6–2 tanks, which would often take water from the columns on the station platform. So monotonous were the visits of the 'tanner-oners' that many train spotters would shout 'scrap it!' when one appeared!

Southall had two freight marshalling yards, east and west of the station, and a constant stream of freight transfer trains passed under the footbridge, many hauled by clanking 'WD' 2–8–0 trains designed by Robert Riddles. The most dramatic freight event of the day, however, was the arrival of the goods train from Brentford Dock. This was hauled up the steep gradient by an 0–6–0 pannier tank and frequently the load appeared to be impossibly heavy. The signalman, possibly out

of sheer devilment, seemed to always manage to stop the train as it approached Southall. The pannier tank would then have to re-start it on the gradient, with several nail-biting seconds elapsing between each explosion of exhaust from the chimney.

Southall engine shed was home mainly to freight locomotives, while the more aristocratic passenger locomotives lived at Old Oak Common shed. Freight locomotives would often finish a spell of duty at Acton marshalling yard, after which three or four locomotives would be coupled together to run along the slow line to Southall. Just east of the footbridge they would stop and wait for a pause in the traffic on the fast lines before being switched onto the crossover to the engine shed side of the main line. This crossover would take them under the footbridge and they would then reverse direction, under the footbridge again, to run into the engine shed yard. As each chimney passed slowly only inches beneath your feet the smells coming through the blackened boards were a heady brew to those hooked on the romance of steam.

This was an urban railway, but Southall nevertheless had its rural anachronism — the '14XX' class 0–4–2 tank engines that worked the auto-trains on the Greenford, Uxbridge and Staines branch lines. These little engines also lived at Southall shed, and their comings and goings among the grimy heavy freight engines evoked holiday memories of the branch lines in Devon and Cornwall.

The attempt to preserve one of them was sparked off by the British Transport Commission's announcement of the list of steam locomotives chosen to be preserved officially. The '14XX', 0–4–2T, which the Southall trainspotters loved so much, did not feature on that list so in April 1961 our four founders decided to send the famous letter to the Editor of the 'Railway Magazine.' By the end of July they had forgotten about it and when the August edition of the magazine was published they were surprised to find themselves in the vanguard of the railway preservation movement.

It is difficult to imagine or recall just how infant the railway preservation 'movement' was in those days. The only schemes at this time which had actually started to operate passenger trains were the narrow gauge Tallyllyn and Festiniog Railways in Wales, and the standard gauge Bluebell Railway. The remainder were all pipe-dreams and there were very few rules. This was just as well, because the committee of the 48XX Preservation Society didn't know any of them anyway!

The advantages they did have on their side were youth, plenty of time and flexibility, which all go hand in hand. When you are 16 years old the future seems infinite, so you do not need to hurry. You are accustomed to learning and not yet set in your ways, so you will alter your objectives to suit the prevailing circumstances. The 48XX Preservation Society had a suitably ambitious objective — to those whose main achievement in life thus far had been to sit 'O' levels — but beyond that the wider aims were vague. "We're going to preserve a '14XX' locomotive," said Angus Davis to the steward on the Bluebell Railway stand at the Model Railway Exhibition, "would you like to have it on your railway?"

"Come back when you've actually bought one and we'll think about it, sonny!" was the disarming reply.

The decision that set the 48XX Preservation Society apart from dozens of similar organisations which never got off the ground, or became absorbed in larger organisations, was the change of name. The inaugural meeting was finally held in Southall Community Centre on May 4 1962, and the people who joined there became members of the fledgling Great Western Preservation Society. At a stroke the infant organisation linked itself inseparably with the Great Western Railway and the traditions and aura surrounding that name.

The original four schoolboys remained predominant on the committee, with Angus Davis as Chairman, Graham Perry as Treasurer and Mike Peart as Secretary. They had been joined in 1961 by Dennis Oldfield and Eric Pascoe. Dennis Oldfield had done much to hold the committee together through the first winter, particularly so one chilly night in December 1961, when a pre-meeting snowball fight turned into fisticuffs! The committee members were on the point of going their separate ways when Dennis told them not to be so damned stupid and to get on with the meeting! Dennis's maturity was further symbolised by the fact that he drove a car while the founder members were still too young to have licences!

During 1962 and early 1963 the committee was strengthened by a number of people whose names will be familiar to many in railway preservation. Among them were Edward Boxell, Peter Lemar, John Pope, Ken Williams and Keith Wilson. Peter Lemar became Chairman after the Society's Annual General Meeting in January 1963, Ken Williams was appointed Publicity Officer, Keith Wilson Membership Secretary and Edward Boxell — who together with Eric Pascoe had served on the Railway Preservation Association — became Committee Secretary. John Pope, a Fleet Street journalist, was appointed Editor of the Newletter, for which the Society's membership had been asked to suggest a title. Amongst the proposals was 'Great Western Echo'. This title was adopted and the first 'Echo' appeared in March 1963 and the format was changed at the same time from foolscap (13in × 8in) to quarto (10 × 8in). Although it was still produced on a duplicating machine, John Pope's skill gave it much of the cachet of an expensively printed magazine. The first printed editions appeared in 1965, and over the years the magazine has developed into an authoritative and highly-regarded magazine devoted to the ways of the GWR.

A fair proportion of the committee's time at this stage was spent in discussing the Society's eventual aim. It was acknowledged that the organisation did not have

GWR '1361' class 0–6–0ST No. 1363, standing alone at Plymouth Laira shed, in 1964. BR's asking price of £700 for this engine was considered to be a major stumbling block at the time! *Frank Dumbleton*.

the resources to buy and run its own branch line, but the committee was reluctant to settle for static preservation in a museum. The Didcot-style Railway Centre so familiar today had yet to be invented!

There were also other problems. It might seem strange today, but in 1963 'preservation' in a railway context was becoming a dirty word. Very few of the railway preservation societies were actually achieving anything concrete and it was felt by some people that the number of organisations in existence was too high to be supported and sustained by the railway enthusiast fraternity.

The reality of the situation was that railway enthusiasts generally were having far too much fun to worry about preservation. The wholesale scrapping of steam locomotives caused by the modernisation of the railways had been accelerated by the closure of thousands of route-miles and hundreds of stations under the Beeching plan. Practically every weekend there would be a last chance to ride behind this class of locomotive, or to travel over that branch line. Any suggestion that money might be spared for preservation was met with hoots of derision. To propose as we did, with cast-iron logic, that if everybody on the raitour put the price of his ticket into a fund they would raise enough money to buy the engine at the front of it, was to invite a stony silence in response as cheques were written for the next 'last chance' extravaganza.

However, if railway enthusiasts were lukewarm about preservation, British Railways were positively unhelpful — understandably so when millions of pounds were being spent on a fleet of diesels which, time after time, were proving less reliable than the steam locomotives they replaced. Meanwhile the haemmorages caused by the 'Beeching Axe' were in full flood. To these self-inflicted wounds was added the deadly stiletto of the newspapers who gleefully reported that the Bluebell Railway, running pensioned off steam locomotives on a line abandoned by BR as being uneconomic, (but conveniently forgetting all the free labour) was showing a profit, while British Railways were losing millions of pounds. It is not surprising that many railway managers became totally opposed to the fledgeling railway preservation schemes. Those who appreciated that a past to be proud of could become a bankable asset were very few and far between. The committee of the Great Western Preservation Society decided that, in the prevailing mood, the word 'Preservation' in its title was doing its cause no good at all. The name 'Great Western Society' was therefore adopted on June 4 1963. With such a pragmatic philosophy it is not surprising that the Society has thrived and survived to celebrate its quarter-century!

The Society went into the railtour business in its own right in 1963, with a tour of the west London suburban branch lines, from Paddington, including Southall–Brentford, West Drayton–Uxbridge, Slough–Windsor and Maidenhead–High Wycombe, via Marlow. There were a few hiccups, such as a pannier tank being substituted for the '61XX' 2–6–2T advertised, and the train failing to call at Ealing Broadway on the outward journey. However, the '61XX' turned up part-way through the tour and the passengers who had chased it in a taxi from Ealing to Southall were pacified, so in the end the event was considered to be a successful debut in the railtour business.

During 1963 the first reports came of an independent plan to preserve the GWR branch line from Totnes to Ashburton, in Devon. This arch-etypal GWR line was potentially an ideal home for an auto-train and the Society soon made contact with Bob Saunders, a leading light in the scheme. An encouraging relationship was formed and negotiations were strengthened following Peter Lemar's move during the autumn of that year to live and work in Devon.

Another Devon-based preservation scheme was mooted at the same time, for the Kingsbridge branch. This got no further than preliminary neg-otiations with local councils before BR let a contract for the demolition of the track and steel bridges and that was the end of that idea. The pro-poser of this scheme was the late T.W.E. Roche, who was to play an important part, a couple of years later, in the Society's progress nearer to London.

During the year the '14XX' preservation fund had gradually swelled, until in the autumn the Society was able to start inspecting all the surviving members of the class to decide which locomotive was in best condition to purchase. Peter Lemar toured the engine sheds where the locomotives were still allocated, collecting reports from crews and shed staff. David Rouse, a society member then living in North Wales, gave valuable advice on the points to look for generally in assessing a steam locomotive, and later inspected the actual locomotives concerned when a short-list had been drawn up.

A lot of time was also spent in 1963, in an attempt to preserve the last surviving Swindon-built saddle tank, 0–6–0 No. 1363, built in 1910. This started with an offer made by a member at the AGM to purchase the locomotive and loan it to the Society. The individual concerned was rapidly invited to discuss the matter further with the committee. No. 1363 was inspected and, with the Society's interest noted, stored under cover at Plymouth Laira shed. Eventually the selling price was the stumbling block, with BR's quote of £700 being considered too high by our benefactor, who dropped out of the scheme. There was a constant suspicion at the time that BR was quoting prices to railway preservat-ionists far in excess of those a scrap merchant would pay for the hard-ware concerned. Certainly, BR's prices varied quite considerably, with the original 1961 estimate of £1,350 for a '14XX' 0–4–2T being reduced as the Society's bona-fides were established to BR's satisfaction.

Above, left: The four founder members of the GWS, reunited at Didcot in 1985, 150th anniversary year of the GWR. Left to right: Angus Davis, Graham Perry, Mike Peart and Jon Barlow. Above, right: the late T.W.E. Roche, *Both: Frank Dumbleton*

By the end of 1963 the Society's contacts were good enough for the prices paid by scrap merchants to be made available as a cross-check, and this helped considerably.

Early in 1964 the short list of '14XX' locomotives had been reduced to two — Nos. 1450 and 1466. No. 1450 was considered at this point to be in better condition — but it would not be available for sale for about 12 months, by which time the locomotive's condition might have deteriorated. The proposal that No. 1466 be chosen was therefore put to the Annual General Meeting on February 1 1964 and carried unanimously. At the same meeting David Rouse reported on his carriage preservation plans, which included a fund to preserve 1881-built clerestory saloon No. 9044 (eventually successful, with the coach preserved by the Dowty Railway Preservation Society, at Ashchurch) and 'Dreadnought' No. 3299 (built 1905) which he had discovered being used as sleeping accommodation for restaurant car crews at Newquay. This carriage survives today at Didcot.

Peter Lemar stepped down from the Chairmanship after the 1964 AGM, but remained on the committee as South Western representative, while Ken Williams was elected Chairman in his place. Having hovered on its fringes since the beginning, I was elected to the committee at the 1964 AGM and became Secretary. Indeed, I can take some pride in having served briefly on the committee from its earliest days, in August and September 1961. After that summer holiday I had returned to boarding school and achieved the distinction of being the first person to be expelled — from the Society, not the school! — on account of my inability to attend meetings!

No. 1466 was eventually offered to the Society in February 1964, the price being £750 — delivered! The engine had been withdrawn at Taunton shed and there was no question of it being delivered anywhere else but Totnes. Bob Saunders had offered storage space on a siding in the yard of Staverton Contractors, and it was here that No. 1466 steamed on Wednesday March 18 1964. Driver L. Milford and Fireman A.R. Discombe of Newton Abbot were the footplate crew. Peter Lemar reported an unexpected bonus of "a fairly large selection of tools secreted on various parts of the engine, with certain spare parts, a new shovel, the fire tools, oil can and headlamps." We were in business!

During the following month a group of committee members made their first weekend visit to the engine. Ken Williams drove his new Ford Anglia, with Angus Davis, Graham Perry and myself as passengers. We were invited to lunch with Peter Lemar in Torquay and after the meal he suggested casually that we might steam No. 1466 that afternoon. Such was the relaxed nature of pioneer preservationists! Peter reckoned that he had picked up the rudiments of handling a locomotive from his recent tour of engine sheds and Angus volunteered his experience of driving 5in gauge models at Harlington Locomotive Society! We had intended to clean No. 1466 but steaming the locomotive seemed a much more exciting prospect, so off we went for a course of Teach Yourself Engine Driving. So unprepared were we for a steaming that we arrived at Totnes without even one match between us! Somebody had to be sent to buy a box!

One thing we did learn that afternoon is that you're never alone with a steam engine. As soon as enough steam had been raised to blow the whistle we triumphantly blew it and as the sound echoed around the rooftops of Totnes, people were already hurrying to join in the fun. An old white sheet which had been intended for use as cleaning rags was tied across the gateposts of Staverton's yard, and No. 1466 moved for the first time under the Society's ownership!

Over the May Bank Holiday weekend a gang of Society members converged on Totnes for the first big organised working party. David Rouse had by now been successful in raising funds to buy the 'Dreadnought' and this gigantic carriage had arrived at Totnes a few days earlier. The 'Devonia Guest House' offered a special rate of 15 shillings (75p) a night for bed and breakfast, although hardier souls slept in the 'Dreadnought.' This was tolerably comfortable if you didn't freeze, but ablutions were rudimentary, with the nearest (cold) tap 200 yards away in the open air. The public conveniences were 400 yards in the opposite direction, and those who were lazy, or in a hurry, would drive!

Despite the outward appearance of progress, there was an unease among the committee members which manifested itself in a number of heated exchanges. It is a shock to any organisation when a dream becomes a reality and unexpected responsibilities have to be dealt with. Money would have helped, but this was one of the worries. After the £750 cheque for the '14XX' had been cashed by British Railways the Society had about £80 left in the bank and Graham Perry estimated that £200 would be needed to get through the rest of the year. Either an influx of new members, or cost-cutting, was essential. Imminent expenditure included insurance for No. 1466 while Tony Goss, a splendid new recruit who lived in Totnes, was creating a restoration team of local members who needed tools and materials to keep them occupied. It all cost money, and we were short of it.

I suppose many of us had fondly believed that No. 1466 would very soon be chuffing up and down in the idyllic surroundings of the Dart Valley and earning her living. But very little news was coming from the Dart Valley Railway, and Peter Lemar, who had been taken into the confidence of its committee, certainly wasn't going to jeopardise the Society's position by breaking that confidence. The GWS still had to raise money to preserve an auto-trailer to run with No. 1466, so Peter asked for the committee's blessing for an attempt to preserve 0–6–0ST No. 1363 by personally circulating an appeal to members. It was a case of 'now-or-never' because No. 1363's sanctuary, Laira Shed was about to be demolished and the historic locomotive would then go for scrap.

Perhaps because of resentment at the way Peter was keeping 'mum' over the DVR, the next committee meeting became a heated discussion about the rights and wrongs of No 1363's preservation. Unfortunately Peter could not attend this meeting, but was able to point out at the following gathering that only two committee members had commented on the No. 1363 fund proposal, and both were in favour. As the fund had been an overnight success the committee agreed that it would be churlish not to accept No. 1363 into its care!

Another successful preservation bid this summer saved one of the few remaining clerestory coaches, all-third No. 1941, built in 1901. This was the personal initiative of Society member Arthur Benson, from Cardiff, and restoration of the coach commenced in South Wales. It can be found today at Didcot.

In July 1964 the South West members asked permission to steam No. 1466 so that she could be examined and any faults noted. The committee was not enthusiastic, on grounds of cost, but allowed the steaming to proceed because a BR fitter had agreed to carry out the inspection. In the event the locomotive nearly suffered serious damage. Here's the story.

When the time came to light the fire that day, the person responsible noticed that the firebox had been filled with ashes and dirt by some uncharitable soul. In his inexperience he didn't realise that this would materially affect the steaming ability of the engine, because the flow of air through the firebars would be choked. So he went ahead and lit a fire on top of all the ash and everybody waited and waited while desultory flames flickered in the firebox. Nothing could induce the engine to raise steam. Not even tapping the boiler pressure gauge as if the needle had become stuck like a barometer! The waiting went on for hours and in order to avoid boredom let us take a brief tour of the area of the Society's operations in Totnes. We were located on a siding off the Quay line, which left the main line at Totnes station and, while the Dart Valley line set off northwards, the quay line ran south for about half-a-mile to an area alongside the River Dart, near the town centre, known as 'The Plains.' Goods had been transhipped here in the past, but the line onto the Quay itself had closed. However, about half-way between the station and the Quay a trailing point gave access to a long siding running northwards, back towards the main line. This siding ran alongside a road for most of its length and served a commercial area which had developed on the site of Totnes Racecourse.

The first enterprise reached by the siding was Totnes Cattle Market,

Right: Auto-trailer No. W231W, built by BR in 1951 to a GWR design, was bought by the GWS in 1964 for £300. Still in maroon livery and lined in black-and-straw, the vehicle is seen here paired with No. 1466 during a GWS open day at Totnes on June 26 1965. The purchase of this train marked the achievement of the Society's original aim, but in reality it was only a small beginning. *GWS Collection.*

served by a short siding of its own, parallel to the main siding, for loading and unloading cattle vans. The Market had been built about two years previously and, in the manner we had come to expect, the opening by HM The Queen more or less co-incided with BR's decision to pull out of the livestock distribution market west of Exeter. The 'Dreadnought' coach now resided on the otherwise disused cattle dock siding. A couple of hundred yards further on South Devon Farmers had a warehouse. This created a daily movement of grain wagons which were collected and delivered by a main line diesel-hydraulic locomotive early in the moring. The shunter had a way of nonchalantly banging on the windows of the 'Dreadnought' with his pole and the driver would grin down from his cab at the newly-awakened occupants of the bunks. "Maaarnin' m'dear!" he would cheerfully call.

Finally the siding entered Staverton's yard through a lockable gate, ending in a buffer-stop at the foot of, and at right angles to, the embankment carrying the main line. Here we rejoin the knot of people disconsolately watching a very lifeless No. 1466.

"Steam her on wood!" This shout signalled the last expedient for the frustrated steam-raisers, who then scurried around looking for any pieces of scrap timber. Large pieces were reduced to firebox size in a frenzied attack with a coal pick. If an old bath could be found to fill with inflammable liquid to soak the wood so much the better! Even the most recalcitrant boiler cannot resist this treatment, and No. 1466 had soon raised enough steam to chuff up and down the siding a few times. She was inspected as planned and most of the audience then departed. The

remainder parked the 0–4–2T beside the 'Dreadnought' where the kettle was boiling for tea.

The drama started a few minutes later when somebody looking around the cab noticed that the boiler pressure had dropped to 30 psi. More seriously, the water-level in the gauge glass had also dropped until it was almost out of sight, and with the pressure too low to work the injectors it was impossible to refill the boiler to a safe level. Within a few minutes the water covering the crown of the firebox would boil away and the fusible plug would melt — disaster. A rapid dropping of the fire was essential, but here was another problem. The hot coals could not be shovelled out through the fireman's side of the cab because the 'Dreadnought' was parked right alongside. It had to be 'baled out' of the driver's side which meant that a glowing mound soon built up on the road surface adjacent to the track. It was not difficult to imagine the effect this was having on the tar beneath. When Totnes Borough Council eventually came looking for the culprit who had burnt a pothole in their tarmac road they would put two and two together in no time at all!

However, all was not lost because, just a few yards away, the road crossed a stream. All spare hands gathered any utensil that would carry water and in the gathering dusk they raced to and fro, dashing water on each flaming shovelful as it was dropped out of the side of the cab. Fortunately, this farcical scene did not last long before we were saved by what seemed at the time like a miracle! The contents of the firebox which were being shovelled out so energetically included the ash which had been choking the fire all afternoon. With the ash removed, air

began to flow between the firebars again and the fire burned brighter and brighter. In no time the boiler pressure had risen to 80 pounds, the injectors were started and the boiler water-level rose to a safe level. The crisis being over, a few runs up and down the siding were made in the darkness before No. 1466 was safely locked away in Staverton's yard for the night.

Bliss it was, next morning, to lie on the hard bunk in the 'Dreadnought' and grin back at our friendly driver as he brought the day's grain wagons for South Devon Farmers. What a tale he would have been able to tell his mates if we had been forced to beg him to shunt a crippled No. 1466 into the yard! If you are of a nervous disposition, let me hasten to add that railway preservation has come a long way since those experimental, pioneering days. Like the great Isambard Kingdom Brunel, who had some narrow escapes in the infancy of the Great Western Railway, the only way for the Society to learn was through its own mistakes!

The year's autumn activities included an auto-train railtour from Swindon with an itinerary which covered the closed Calne branch line, Westbury, Bath and Bristol before returning to Swindon via the South Wales cut-off line. The locomotive was No. 1444 and the young fireman had never been on a steam locomotive before! In October an Open Day was held at Totnes with both Nos. 1466 and 1363 — which had arrived in August — in steam.

The Society was now almost in a position to purchase its auto-trailer coach, and No. 231 was selected. Some reservations were voiced at the fact that this post-nationalisation coach had been built by BR in 1951,

The 'pulling power' of the Swindon-built locomotive is amply illustrated in this view of No. 7808 *Cookham Manor*, the centre of attention at the GWS open day at Taplow, on September 15 1966. No. 4079 *Pendennis Castle* is in the background. *Frank Dumbleton*.

but it was agreed that a vehicle in running order should be preserved so that it could enter service on the Dart Valley Railway almost immediately. No. 231 also had the advantage of GWR-style seating, compared with some of the other BR-built auto-trailers, which had tubular framed bus-style seats. BR's price was £400, which seemed surprisingly high, until it was discovered that they had mistakenly quoted for a GWR diesel railcar — and the auto-trailer would be priced at £300!

These successful preservation projects belied the Society's finances which were still in a parlous state, with very little room for manoeuvre. After the £300 cheque had been sent to BR to purchase No. 231 the cash available for expenditure was just under £25. The tension at committee meetings continued, culminating in Ken Williams' resignation in October: his place as Chairman was taken over by Eric Pascoe.

It is true to say that by this time the Great Western Society had outgrown the management committee's ability to administer it efficiently. However, during 1964 the membership had increased from 200 to 400 and with this number were several individuals who were willing to form local groups in order to further the Society's aims. An unofficial South West committee had been formed during the summer and the South West Group was officially inaugurated on February 20 1965, at Totnes. The venue for the meeting was the newly-delivered auto-trailer No. 231 and during that afternoon the Totnes collection was augmented with the arrival of 0–6–0 pannier tank No. 1369, which had been preserved by a fund organised by Group committee member Alan Weary.

Regional groups were also formed at this time in Reading, Swindon, Bristol and South Wales. However, in London a 'Branch' was formed (the GWR had branches, not groups, its committee maintained!) and Ken Williams took an active role in the social events for members, the Groups were able to take on fund-raising activities. The traction engine movement was just beginning to 'take off' at this time and the blossoming number of rallies provided valuable outlets for Group sales stands. National Council meetings were an inspired innovation which gave the group and management committees a chance to meet and discuss problems and progress. The first 'NCM' was held in June 1965 and with the representatives voicing their opinions in accents emanating from all parts of the GWR system, it proved how widespread the support for our Society was becoming.

The Society's preservation activity in 1965 was dominated by the fund to preserve a GWR two-cylinder mixed traffic 4–6–0. The four-cylinder 4–6–0s would be represented by the preservation of No. 6000 *King George V* — which was BR's avowed intention — and No. 4073 *Caerphilly Castle*, already in London's Science Museum. 4079 *Pendennis Castle* had also been preserved by Mike Higson, with the Society assisting him in the negotiations. But there were no moves — official or unofficial — to preserve a 'Hall', 'Manor' or 'Grange' 4–6–0. The Society therefore costed out the scrap value of all three classes, giving the following figures: 'Hall' — £1,852, 'Grange' — £2,085 and 'Manor' — £1,826. The 'Grange' price was higher because of the larger proportion of non-ferrous metals used in its construction. The Society membership was therefore asked to choose between a 'Manor' and a 'Hall'. Of the 259 members who replied, 200 were in favour of a 'Hall', 52 wanted a 'Manor' and 2 didn't mind which 4–6–0 was chosen, while 5 were opposed to the fund as a whole. This early example of preservation market research resulted in a 'Hall' Fund being launched by the GWS in August 1965.

By this time, the siding space available at Totnes was fully occupied and the Dart Valley Railway had not yet been given authority to store any stock on their line. Consequently, alternative sites for the temporary storage of stock were being considered. One possibility was Taplow goods shed which the Reading Group had rented as a club house, thanks to T.W.E. Roche. 'TWE', who will be remembered as the instigator of the abortive Kingsbridge branch preservation scheme in 1963, had been elected to the Reading Group committee. His friendship with the Western Region's London Divisional Manager, David Pattisson, gave the Society the ear of a senior — and sympathetic — railwayman for the first time. David Pattison fortunately, was one of the few managers who appreciated the commercial advantages to BR of supporting railway preservation.

When 'TWE' proposed holding a Reading Group Open Day at Taplow, David Pattison and his Public Relations Officer, Don Rubber, entered into the arrangements with great gusto. It was agreed that *Pendennis Castle* could move from Southall shed, where it was stored, to Taplow for the day and that two BR diesels would also be exhibited. The Open Day event, in September 1965, was a fantastic success, with 1,500 visitors. Moreover, it altered the Society's whole outlook on Open Days, which until then had been considered more or less as a service to members, and not as profit-making events. Nevertheless, we were expecting a good crowd for the next Totnes Open Day on October 2 when *Pendennis Castle* was booked to haul a railtour from Paddington to Exeter. From Exeter to Totnes the train would be double-headed by Collett 0–6–0 No. 3205 and 2–6–2T No. 4555, which were both destined for preservation on the Dart Valley Railway. The railtour would continue from Totnes to Plymouth behind a diesel locomotive, so we were confident that most of the passengers would choose to remain at Totnes and visit the Society's Open Day before being picked up to return to London.

Permission had at last been given for stock to be stored at Buckfastleigh on the Dart Valley line, and the newly arrived locomotives were scheduled to move straight there, taking with them four auto-trailer coaches which had been bought by the Dart Valley company and which were waiting at Totnes station. From our siding we heard the whistling as the train arrived at Totnes and expected that within a few minutes we would be entertaining our visitors. Nobody arrived. Eventually word reached us that, when Nos. 3205 and 4555 were uncoupled from the railtour coaches, they were each coupled to two of the auto-trailers ready to move to Buckfastleigh. No sooner had this happened that the passengers from the railtour climbed aboard for the ride up the weed-overgrown, tree-overhung branch line. With No. 3205 running tender-first her cab roof acted like a scythe, lopping off the lower branches. The crew kept the footplate clear by feeding them into the firebox! Having arrived at Buckfastleigh, and the bus service to Totnes being nothing to write home about, it was then agreed that 3205 and her auto-trailers would run the passengers back to Totnes in time to catch their train home.

Even now No 3205 was on her way, so most of the Society officials abandoned their Open Day and hurried to the station to ride back to Buckfastleigh behind 3205! This unexpected bonus tempered the frustration of organising an Open Day which nobody visited! In the event, this episode proved to be even more of a milestone, for it happened to be the first occasion that the Directors of the Dart Valley Railway Company, as it now was, were introduced to the high-spirited, youthful members of the Great Western Society's management committee 'en masse', so to speak. We later learned that the impression some of them gained of our organisation was, in a word, 'irresponsible'. This was apparently on account of the bowler hat which Graham Perry wore! Although it would be irresponsible to blame Graham's hat for the eventual decision that the GWS and the Dart Valley Railway would go their separate ways, Peter Lemar did observe at the time: "If they will not allow this sort of thing we can well suspect what other things they may frown upon." Incidentally, as the respected middle-aged Chairman of the Great Western Society today, Graham Perry still wears his bowler hat on ceremonial occasions!

At least, after the frustrating years of inactivity, the Dart Valley Railway scheme was making progress, although the role which our Society might be offered was still uncertain. The DVR Company had indicated that it would wish to take control of No. 1466 and auto-coach No. 231, either by cash purchase or in exchange for shares. The remainder of the Society's stock could be accommodated on the line but it would not be regularly used. In November 1965 the Dart Valley Railway Association was formed, taking over what might have been the Great Western Society's role as the enthusiasts' support body. At the same time, two Directors of the Dart Valley Railway Company advised that an individual was interested in purchasing a 'Hall' 4–6–0 and asked the Great Western Society to hold off with its own bid for a member of this class.

This request put the GWS management committee in a quandary. Twenty years ago the accepted view was that the sum total of GWR branch line preservation would be the Dart Valley Railway, which would have to be operated by small locomotives, as the track was just not sufficiently heavily engineered to take large locomotives. While BR had not yet banned preserved steam locomotives from hauling main line railtours, it was expected to be only a matter of time before this happened. In these circumstances it was expected that the larger classses would have limited use in preservation and that the best course of action would be to keep one representative example of as many types as possible. Would posterity thank us if we ended up with two 'Halls' preserved, while other classes went to extinction? Would those who had donated cash been happy to see it put into a duplication? Would it not be better if the Society was to turn its attention to a 'Manor' 4–6–0 instead?

On the other hand the Society's membership had voted overwhelmingly in favour of preserving a 'Hall', had raised the money and in a subsequent ballot had chosen No. 6998 *Burton Agnes Hall* with 1,095 votes, against 14 for No. 6959 *Peatling Hall* and 87 for No. 6923 *Croxteth Hall*. So, there was a clear mandate to purchase No. 6998 *Burton Agnes Hall* and this engine was due to be withdrawn within a few weeks. Twenty years ago, BR's policy still held good that a locomotive sold to a scrap merchant could not be re-sold for preservation. Posterity would certainly not thank us if every 'Hall' was scrapped after all the effort which had been put into the fund. Being so close to success, the Society decided to go ahead with its own proposal.

The recent changes in our relationship with the Dart Valley Railway had given the committee food for thought, in that maybe the Society's best interests would be served by setting up on its own, and consideration of alternative sites began. Society membership had again doubled during 1965, to total

Left: Class '61XX' 2–6–2T No. 6106 (built 1931) stands at Henley on Thames station on June 24 1967 *Frank Dumbleton*.

800 by the end of the year, and with this size of support, an independent existence could be seriously contemplated.

On January 3 1966, No. 6998 *Burton Agnes Hall* became the last steam locomotive to haul a scheduled passenger train on the Western Region, from Oxford to Banbury. The Society's bid of £2,500 was accepted and the locomotive waited at Oxford shed for delivery instructions. Why, you may well ask, did the Society pay £2,500 when only the previous summer the price had been calculated as £1,852? The answer is that in 1965 Rhodesia made its Unilateral Declaration of Independence; economic sanctions had halted the flow of copper from Zambia, through the Rhodesian ports, and the price of the metal soared. There's an awful lot of copper in a steam locomotive and scrap prices soared in sympathy!

While the outcome of the 'Hall' fund was being decided, Peter Lemar made contact with the late Professor John Mynors, then living in Iraq, who offered to buy a 'Manor' 4–6–0; on the condition that the GWS succeeded in preserving a 'Hall' and assuming that a 'Manor' could be found in reasonable working order. At the same time, David Rouse was negotiating on behalf of another expatriate, D.R. Gwynne-Jones, to purchase 2–6–2T 6106. Both were successful: No. 7808 *Cookham Manor* was purchased from Gloucester shed and moved to the Dowty Railway Preservation Society base at Ashchurch, while in April, No. 6106 was moved from Southall shed to Taplow. By April, BR was becoming anxious to move No. 6998 *Burton Agnes Hall* from Oxford and the 4–6–0 was steamed and ran under its own power to Totnes. To make room for the engine on the cattle dock siding Nos. 1369, 1466 and auto-coach 231 were moved to Buckfastleigh. Two more coaches were preserved by the South West Group of the GWS and also moved to Buckfastleigh: No 7372, a Hawksworth Brake Composite (built 1948) and No. 5952, a Collett all-third built in 1935. No. 5952 had a fortunate escape when it was already marshalled into a rake of coaches at Plymouth, waiting to go for a scrap. David Rouse happened to be passing in a bus when he caught a glimpse of it. At this time David was working as a conductor for the Western National Company, so he stopped the bus and carried out a swift inspection. With the bus now running late David decided that a few minutes more delay wouldn't matter, so he made a call to Peter Lemar from a wayside telephone box, asking him to use his contacts to get no. 5952 uncoupled from the train while there was still time to save it from the scrapman.

The Society event which outshone all others in 1966 was the September Open Day at Taplow. The attractions we'd offered the previous year were augmented by passenger rides in 'Ocean Saloon' coaches behind No. 6106, and No. 7808 *Cookham Manor* paid a visit with a railtour from Birmingham. Once again attendances exceeded the wildest expectations, with 6,000 visitors coming through the gate. Taplow was just too small to handle this sort of crowd, while BR's charges for moving locomotives there just for the one day swallowed up a large proportion of the revenue. What the Society needed was a site where the attractions could be permanently exhibited, with plenty of space, — and easily accessible to the large population of London and the Thames Valley. That is how Didcot eventually came to be focussed upon.

Relations with the Western Region's London Division remained excellent. For the Society's Annual General Meetings, held at Bristol in 1966 and 1967, it was arranged that members travelled in 'Ocean Saloon' coaches attached to service trains from Paddington. From 1966 the Society rented the former Station Master's Office at West Ealing station as its administrative headquarters. Here, in February 1967, the Articles of Association were signed which turned the Society into a limited company: yet another step towards maturity.

Early in 1967, the Society's Bristol Group were successful with an appeal to save '56XX' 0–6–2T No. 6697 which joined *Cookham Manor* at Ashchurch. No. 6106 continued to perform regularly at Taplow and was even allowed to steam to Henley-on-Thames for a weekend in June. By now, the move to Didcot was becoming a real option. *Pendennis Castle* was already stored in the lifting shop there, having been sold by Mike Higson to W.H. McAlpine and John Gretton. David Pattisson was also anxious for the Society to move somewhere less visible from the main line. He had suffered an embarrassing experience when travelling through Taplow with his General Manager. "Funny," said the GM as he caught sight of No. 6106, "I thought we had scrapped all those!"

Before the move to Didcot there was one last blockbuster Taplow Open Day in September 1967. *Pendennis Castle* made its third visit and our old friend No. 3205 also appeared. That engine had been transferred by David Rouse from Buckfastleigh to the developing Severn Valley Railway. Apart from being an attraction at the Open Day it would also take the 'Ocean Saloon' No. 9113 *Prince of Wales* back to Bridgnorth. The other two 'Ocean

Saloons' at Taplow had also been preserved, No. 9112 *Queen Mary* by a Society member, the late Dr John Dorling, and No. 9118 *Princess Elizabeth* by the Reading Group of the Society. The indefatigable David Rouse was 'hawking' raffle tickets for his next project — the rescue of '43XX' 2–6–0 No. 5322 from Barry Scrapyard. He had finally breached BR's rule that locomotives sold for scrap must be cut up, on account of the historic importance of No. 5322 as the last surviving Churchward 'Mogul'.

A useful workforce had formed at Taplow and they were eager to get to grips with more ambitious projects at Didcot. Some were a new generation of schoolboys — Joe Carter, Mick Cranswick, Ashley Jones, Dave Roberts, Mike Sanderson and Ralph Wiltshire. Others brought engineering experience, like Fred Graves and Des Lauder. Paddy Baker could always be relied on for an apposite comment or a risqué joke.

The move from Taplow was set for Saturday November 4 when No. 6106 ran light engine to Kensington Olympia first of all, to pick up two Pullman Cars which were to be stored at Didcot before being shipped to the USA for preservation. Back at Taplow the 'Ocean Saloons,' Nos. 9112 and 9118, were collected together with a BR utility van full of spare parts. Next call was Didcot itself where No. 6106 left the coaches, took water and proceeded to Oxford where two more vehicles destined for the USA were waiting. These were LNER sleeping cars which had apparently been used by General Eisenhower during the Second World War. They certainly smelled as if they hadn't been cleaned since then!

That morning Paddy Baker and I had stood on the bridge at Taplow station while two sleek Maidenhead maidens rode their horses beneath us. "Remarkable," observed Paddy, "How girls always grow to resemble their pets!" The same afternoon in the drizzling winter dusk our first view of Didcot was the football field, where a few disconsolate knots of spectators watched the match. In the background the slate grey roofs of the terraced houses in Station Road merged with the mist as they marched up the hill towards the town centre. It seemed a long way from the riverside 'chic' of Taplow. Would we ever get to love this place?

A month later, on Saturday December 2, the stock moved from Devon in what was probably the most extraordinary preserved cavalcade ever to be permitted on British Railways metals. The previous week all the stock to be included in the epic journey had been moved from Totnes and Buckfastleigh to Plymouth, to be prepared for its long trip. It had been agreed that Nos. 1363 and 7372 would find a home at Bodmin and the contributors to No. 1369's rescue had voted for her to remain on the Dart Valley Railway. From Plymouth No. 6998 *Burton Agnes Hall* was in the lead, with No. 1466 behind her, more or less along for the ride. The crew hardly dared open 1466's regulator beyond the minimum position for lubrication, for fear of running short of water between stops! The coaches were filled with the Society's stock of spares together with the hardier souls among the membership who had paid for the ride. At Newton Abbot the Carriage & Wagon examiner decided that the 'Dreadnought' was unfit to continue, whereupon Peter Lemar asked him if he was prepared to justify that decision to the Divisional Manager on Monday morning. The 'Dreadnought' carried on, giving no problem — apart from the lavatory door lock coming apart, trapping Peter inside!

As dusk fell, the only lights inside the train were Tilley lamps swinging in the ceilings of two 'Dreadnought' compartments. At Newbury a huge crowd was waiting on the station and the lights in the 'Dreadnought' served to emphasise its bulk against the darkened windows of the other coaches.

I don't recall any feeling of 'coming home' when we finally arrived at Didcot that evening. Years of neglect had made the engine shed and its yard a forlorn place, and several more years would pass before the Great Western Society had resources to get to grips with the backlog of maintenance. Conventional wisdom still had it that branch line preservation was the only worthwhile aim, but the branch lines had yet to tackle the problem of keeping a locomotive fleet running by disfiguring idyllic stations with engine sheds. And Didcot had yet to prove that the most idyllic branch line station could be successfully and attractively created in a corner of an engine shed yard. It is a station that fulfills the schoolboy dreams of a quarter of a century ago and which when the last auto-train has left in the evening, is enjoyed in the stillness by the rabbits and the rambling roses.

As it was in the Great Western, is now.

On Saturday December 2 1967, 'Hall' 4–6–0 No. 6998 *Burton Agnes Hall* tackles Dainton Bank, leading No. 1466 and three GWS-owned vehicles away from Devon, en route to Didcot, the location for the next major phase of the Society's development. *Peter W. Gray.*

CHAPTER 2

DIDCOT 1840–1967

Michael H.C. Baker

With the name 'Flying Star' chalked on the upper half of its smokebox door, Collett side-window cab 2-6-0 No. 9317 passes Didcot on August 16 1936 with a 12-coach passenger train which includes two clerestory roofed vehicles at the rear of the formation. *H.C. Casserley*

THE first steam train reached Didcot in 1840, and despite rumours to the contrary none of the crew or passengers is to be found at the Centre today! Timekeeping may not always have been 100%, and as Adrian Vaughan recalls in his book 'Grub, Water and Relief', in those early days snowdrifts and floods could cause trains to be horribly delayed, but even those passengers forced to sit inches deep in storm water, to the amusement of railwaymen at Reading and Didcot, or who took 9¾ hours one January night in 1841 to overcome flood and landslide between Reading and Paddington, all eventually reached their destinations.

In those days of course, the trains ran on Brunel's broad gauge, (7ft 0¼") and although travel for the poor, despised, third-class customer could be pretty miserable, for the first and second-class travellers it could be a fine experience. By the early 1850s, when Gooch's celebrated 'Iron Duke Singles' were in charge of the principal expresses, the 'Exeter Flier', to which no third-class passengers were admitted, was covering the 53 miles from Paddington to Didcot in 55 minutes. This made it the fastest train in Britain — or anywhere else — and ever since then Didcot has basked in

the glory of its position astride one of the great racing stretches of the railway world.

Churchward's superb 'Saint' and 'Star' 4–6–0s re-asserted the Great Western Railway's superiority in the Edwardian era, and their successors, the 'Castle', 4–6–0s of C.B. Collett, had by 1929 taken charge of the 'Cheltenham Flyer' and were running the 77.3 miles from Swindon to Paddington at a start-to-stop average speed of 66.3 mph. Once again, the GWR possessed the fastest train in the world. The record was held by No. 5006 *Tregenna Castle*, which in June 1932 brought the time down to 56 minutes 47 seconds. The 4–6–0 averaged 39 miles of that run, including the section through Didcot, at 90 mph, and 81.7 mph overall, which to this day remains a record for British steam traction. Surprisingly, the highest speed reached by No. 5006 was only 92 mph, and it wasn't until a few weeks before the outbreak of World War II that the first fully authenticated 100 mph speed (not

withstanding City of Truro's claim of May 1904) was logged on GWR metals. On July 31 1939, No. 4086 *Builth Castle* had charge of the 12.45pm Paddington - Worcester, which passed Didcot by way of the East curve, as Oxford and Worcester trains still do today, and stopped only at Kingham. Accelerating away from this stop the magic '100' was reached on the run down Campden Bank. Almost certainly both 'Castles' and 'Kings' reached 100 mph at other times and in other locations before 1939, and once track and locomotive standards returned to their pre–1939 high levels of maintenance after World War II, and especially in the final years of double-chimney draughting improvements, there were probably many occasions more when three figures were achieved.

The 'Bristolian' was more commonly associated with the 'century' speed than any other train, although what would seem to be the highest authentic speed recorded with Great Western steam was actually achieved away from the Didcot line, when 108.5 mph was recorded near Patney by the 'Cornish Riviera' in the charge of 4–6–0 No. 6015 *King Richard III* in September 1955. Twenty years later Didcot got its 'revenge' when on a trial run in

Above: The down 'Cornishman' (10.15am Paddington–Penzance) at Cholsey on March 24 1894, nearly two years after the abolition of the broad gauge, in the charge of a 'Sir Daniel' class 2–2–2 express locomotive. The 7ft. 0¼in. 'baulk road' has been narrowed to 4ft 8½in.

Right: The end of Brunel's broad gauge. The last broad gauge down 'Cornishman', hauled by 4–2–2 *Great Western*, dashes past Didcot East on May 20 1892.
Both: Great Western Trust.

the summer of 1975 the gas-turbine powered prototype Advanced Passenger Train howled through at a speed approaching 2½ miles a minute, touching 151 mph at one point on its journey from Reading to Swindon.

Nowadays, the highest speeds ever achieved by Great Western steam in its prime are surpassed many times every day as Inter City HSTs speed east and west non-stop through Didcot. HSTs also call at Didcot, bringing it regularly within 45 minutes of Paddington and an hour of Bristol. I don't think a survey has ever been done of the proportion of visitors who arrive at the Didcot Railway Centre by rail, but it must be higher than for practically all other steam centres. Nevertheless, the great majority of Didcot station's customers are commuters. Oxford has a good passenger service to London, but Didcot has better links

and many of the inhabitants on the southern side of the university city and its environs recognising this drive to Didcot to travel by rail. The dual carriageway A34 trunk road provides excellent access and British Rail has exploited this asset to the full. An extensive new car park on the site of the historic provender store was opened in 1984, and in 1985 a lavish and attractive rebuilding of the station, with much use of red brick, with a travel centre, resulted in the station being renamed 'Didcot Parkway'.

How great have been the changes in the 146 years of Didcot's railway

history? The HST's 45-minute schedule between Paddington and Didcot, admittedly with a short stop at Reading, is only ten minutes faster than the broad gauge 'Exeter Flier' of 1850! And when I was stationed at RAF Abingdon in 1956 I would sometimes catch a train which left Oxford around teatime and reached Paddington non-stop in exactly an hour; it was usually entrusted to a 'Hall' 4–6–0. This was considered to be really high-speed travel, yet it represented an average speed of only some 5 mph greater than that of 1850! The difference was, of course, that the 1850 service weighed little

Left: A 4–4–2 'County' tank (class 2200) stands at Didcot with an up train. This class, which had previously monopolised London suburban traffic, was displaced and made extinct in the early 1930s by the arrival of the '6100' 2–6–2Ts. The 4–4–2Ts, with their limited tractive effort, had been losing ground to road competition. *GWS Collection.*

Below: A 'Bulldog' 4-4-0 runs between Tilehurst and Pangbourne with a Birkenhead–Bournemouth through service, circa 1930. *GWS Collection*

more than 100 tons, — including engine, tender and train, but it does demonstrate the potential of the broad gauge.

Even more remarkable than this was a special which Daniel Gooch organised in 1848 and which covered the 53 miles from Paddington to Didcot in 47½ minutes behind one of his 'Iron Duke' 'Singles.' Truly startling stuff. The 'Iron Dukes', and their cosmetically improved, but essentially identical successors, monopolised Great Western expresses between Paddington and Bristol until the end of the broad gauge in 1892. Although *Lord of the Isles* was sadly scrapped in 1905 after being set aside for many years,

the Science Museum, which had refused the Great Western's offer of her, made handsome amends for the GWR's 150th anniversary by building a working reproduction *Iron Duke* using parts of a former NCB Hunslet 'Austerity' 0-6-0ST. This visited Didcot briefly during its extensive tour of that year and it is due to reappear in 1986 to work on the authentic broad gauge rails laid in Didcot Railway Centre.

Despite all the glamorous and famous locomotives which sped past Didcot in the 125 years of main line steam traction the depot itself was not normally associated with exalted thoroughbreds. In 1921, for example, its 29 locomotives consisted of eleven 0–6–0STs, six Armstrong

0–6–0s, three Dean '2301' 0–6–0s and nine 2–4–0s. Worthy machines each one, no doubt, but none built since the death of good Queen Victoria 20 years earlier! They worked local services, both goods and passenger, to Oxford, Reading, Newbury and Winchester and ventured further afield when the opportunity arose, or shunted the local yards. The shed itself dated from broad gauge times, from 1857, replacing an earlier wooden structure of 1844.

By the 1930s the shed was overdue for replacement and with the aid of Government funds, chiefly provided to relieve unemployment, the present structure (now home of the GWS) was constructed. The old site, immediately north of the goods yard,

Above: 'The Cheltenham Flyer', with a 'Castle' 4–6–0 in charge, lives up to its name west of Didcot, circa 1932. At this time the 'Cheltenham Flyer' was the fastest train in the world, with a start-to-stop average speed in excess of 66 mph. *GWS Collection*.

was abandoned and given over to the goods department, and the new steel-framed, brick-walled, asbestos-clad building situated alongside the east curve began operations in June 1932.

Until the end of the First World War Didcot had been the most easterly member of the large Swindon District, but in 1918 a system of divisions was set up, seven in all, and Didcot, along with Oxford, became part of the Paddington Division. From then on Didcot engines carried two stencilled codes, 'DID', and the divisional 'PDN'. Later on, in 1932 the year the new shed was built, a system of number codes was introduced, although these were for record purposes only and they were not actually carried by the engines. The London Division, quite naturally, became No. 1 which meant that all its sheds had numbers ending in 1. Aylesbury was No. 11 on account of 'A' being the first letter of the alphabet and was thus the lowest numbered shed on the GWR, a singular distinction for a very minor establishment which housed just one locomotive and was merely a sub-shed of Slough.

In this new scheme, Didcot became No. 41, and this time (1932) it kept a motherly eye on three sub-sheds at Lambourn, Newbury and Winchester, which each housed one locomotive, although the Newbury engine had every reason to feel hard done by for it had to be stabled out in the open; in 1938 it was a Dean 'Goods'. Winchester also had an 0–6–0 at this time, whilst Lambourn had a '19XX' 0–6–0T, as it had in 1921.

Didcot's own allocation had increased to 43 locomotives by 1938 and, inevitably, had been modernised somewhat. But there were still plenty of veterans around. For example, there were two saddle tanks, Nos 1925 and 2007, which eventually became the very last of the enormous number of standard Wolverhampton and Swindon standard inside-cylinder 0–6–0STs to remain in service, No. 2007 going for scrap in December 1949, and No. 1925 being withdrawn in April 1951, the rest all having been scrapped or converted into pannier tanks. They were survived by the five Churchward outside cylinder 0–6–0ST dock

'Bulldog' 4–4–0 No. 4103 *Samson* awaits its next duty in Didcot shed yard, in 1930. *L&GRP; Courtesy David & Charles*.

Above: In customary clean condition, 'Barnum' 2–4–0 No. 3210 is stabled at Didcot shed, circa 1930. Note the individual brass numbers attached to the rear splasher. *L&GRP; courtesy David & Charles.*

tanks of 1910, one of which, No. 1363, is preserved at Didcot.

To return to the 1938 scene, there were two old Swindon-built pannier tanks, Nos 1565 and 2783, three from Wolverhampton, Nos 1743, 2076, 79, one modern Collett 0–6–0PT No. 7407 (which at barely two years old was the newest locomotive on the Didcot payroll) eight Dean Goods 0–6–0s Nos 2395/2423/30/2532/3/49/66/71, and four of their successors, Collett '2251's Nos 2259/80/2/5. The 2–4–0s of 1921 had been replaced by 'Duke', 'Bulldog' and 'Earl' Class 4–4–0s, (11 in all) which virtually monopolised the Winchester line, but which were also to be found on local passenger and pick-up goods traffic on the lines to Reading and Oxford.

The 'Dukes' were Nos 3254/6/66

and 3280, the 'Bulldogs' Nos 3377,3419/30/48 and 54, whilst the 'Earls' were Nos 3206 and 3215. If these latter engines are considered as new rather than the rebuilds which they really were, then No. 3215 was even more recent that No. 7407, having emerged from Swindon in October 1937. There was one 'Mogul', a Collett engine, No. 9312, and one big passenger tank. This latter was No. 6106, no less, which as recorded elsewhere was the very

On March 19 1961, Riddles 'Austerity' 2–8–0 No. 90312 is stabled at Didcot, in company with the expected GWR allocation. *Norman Glover.*

first GWS preserved locomotive to take up — or in this case resume — residence, in 1967. There was one other period, in 1962, when No. 6106 was at Didcot in store and might well have then gone for breaking-up. Instead it received a heavy overhaul at Swindon and re-entered service, working from Southall. Finally on the 1938 allocation, there was the depot's sole 4–6–0, No. 5934 *Kneller Hall*.

Didcot had long been an important junction, but from September 1939 it became absolutely vital to the Allied war effort. Vast amounts of supplies and men passed through the station on their way to Southampton, and the sleepy Didcot, Newbury & Southampton line saw undreamt-of traffic, and the depot played host to locomotives from all the 'Big Four' companies in addition to those built by the War Department and in the USA for service in Europe and elsewhere.

In 1947, the last year of the GWR's existence, the allocation of locomotives had risen once again, to 49. In addition to petrol service locomotive No. 26, there were 11 pannier tanks, chiefly engaged on shunting at the ordnance depot at Milton, all but two of this group were Collett engines, the exceptions being Dean examples Nos 907/1861. The Colletts were '57XX' class Nos 3622/3709/ 3721/4601/5710/35/44/52/7710. The 'Dean Goods' engines at the shed had been reduced to the solitary No. 2532 while Collett '2251s' numbered eight, these being Nos 2202/21/26/40/89/ 3210/1/2. A 2–4–0 had returned, MSWJ No. 1334, and there were still seven 4–4–0s 'Duke' No. 9083, 'Bull-dogs' Nos 3376/96/3408/48 and 'Earls' Nos 9006/15. Didcot was one of the last strongholds of 4–4–0s on the Western Region, certainly outside

the Cambrian lines. The allocation of large tender engines had increased dramatically during the War years and in 1947 there were nine 'Moguls', Nos 4318/26/5330/80/81/6329/59/79. One of the only two of this class to have been preserved, No. 5322, is at Didcot today. There were four 'Halls', in 1947, Nos 5905/35/6923/52, and the really heavy brigade was represented by four 2–8–2Ts, Nos 7204/14/ 28/52 and three WD 2–8–0s Nos 70843(90327), 79303(90725) and 78522(90367).

The motive power picture did not change dramatically during steam's remaining years, although the 4–4–0s disappeared, except for the well-remembered reappearance of No. 3440 of *City of Truro*, in 1957. Towards the end of WR steam traction, two-cylinder 4–6–0s came to dominate Didcot's allocation. In the summer of 1965 there were 23 steam engines left at Didcot and of these four were 'Grange' 4–6–0s and no less than 11 were 'Hall' 4–6–0s. It always seemed rather surprising that in a part of the Western Region where '6100s' were so commonplace, Didcot seldom had more than one and often none of the class based at its shed. Nevertheless, as steam approached the end of its days when they had been displaced by DMUs on the suburban services out of Paddington, there were five, Nos 6108/ 10/11/26 and 6154. Finally there were still three 'panniers'. Well, not quite finally, for there were also eight 0–6–0 diesel shunters, of the present

day Class 08. These were the only diesels ever officially allocated to Didcot shed. The big main line diesel — hydraulic types, 'Warships', 'Hymeks', even 'Westerns' and the Brush Class 47s were seen on the depot but they led a lifestyle utterly different to that of the steam locomotive. They could work infinitely longer hours without refuelling and their maintainance needs were a world apart from those of the steam engine, which could be housed anywhere from tiny little one-road sheds such as at Wallingford where a branch '14XX' 0–4–2T was in residence, to the sprawling Old Oak Common shed with its 232 occupants. From now on proper fully-equipped locomotive depots would be reduced to a mere handful. Didcot officially closed in June 1965, although a few dead steam engines remained there in store for some months, and diesels were still using it as a stabling point when No. 6106 arrived on November 4 1967 to open the preservation era.

Below: Hawksworth 'County' 4–6–0 No. 1011 *County of Chester* takes Didcot west curve with a Stephenson Locomotive Society Special, September 20 1964. *Gerald Robinson*.

CHAPTER 3

THE DEVELOPMENT OF DIDCOT AS A RAILWAY CENTRE

Michael H.C. Baker

THERE is a school of thought, or perhaps more of a 'gricer's philosophy', which reckons that the only really authentic steam centre is one which is inches deep in ashes, grease and rust, and where most of the locomotives are either semi-derelict or if the locomotives are complete they must be so filthy that neither name nor number can be distinguished. But it soon became obvious to the GWS that if Didcot was to succeed in recreating as much of the old Great Western Railway atmosphere as it could, a lot of people would have to be cajoled into paying their entrance fee and thus provide the funds needed to make the dream come true. So the site had to look presentable, while dirt and slovenly attitudes had to be banished. Essential needs included clean toilets, an appetising restaurant, a well-stocked book and

souvenir shop and easy and safe access around the shed site. Along with these basic requirements we needed to produce as wide a re-creation of the Great Western scene as possible — a day at Didcot should send enthusiast and family away satisfied that they had enjoyed value-for-money entertainment — and wished to return another day.

At first however, the depot was open only to members, but the first public open day was held on September 20 1969, thus establishing the now-familiar Didcot tradition of a big event, with as many attractions and engines in steam as possible, at the end of the summer season. Two Great Western engines were in steam on that day in 1969, Nos. 1466 and 6106, plus the industrial 0–4–0ST *Bonnie Prince Charlie*, which had arrived from Dibles wharf, Southampton, that

Above: Stabled around the Didcot turntable on September 25 1982 are, (left to right): '1361' class 0–6–0ST No. 1363, '43XX' class 2–6–0 No. 5322 and '56XX' 0–6–2T No. 6697. *Peter Treloar*

summer. In those early days there was no physical boundary between the preservation area and BR sidings and running lines, and looking back we shudder somewhat at pictures of open day events with small boys standing seemingly only inches away from 'Westerns' and 'Warships' thundering by on the East Curve! Nevertheless, no harm came to anyone and it did have the advantage that BR was able to take an active part in Society events, often sending along items of rolling stock for display.

Right: The first GWS locomotive to arrive at Didcot, '61XX' 2–6–2 No. 6106 (built 1931), stands just outside the shed, flanked by a pair of BR class 47 diesel-electrics, in 1967. *Michael H.C. Baker.*

Below: Didcot Railway Centre, September 29 1984. The impressive line-up includes 'Terrier' 0–6–0T No. 32670, '57XX' 0–6–0PT No. 3738, '14XX' 0–4–2T No. 1466, GWR 4–4–0 3217 *Earl of Berkeley* and LMS '5XP' 4–6–0 No. 5690 *Leander. Brian Stephenson.*

One of the first Didcot occupants of the preservation era was GWR diesel railcar No. 4. The GWR pioneered, along with the Great Northern Railway of Ireland, the successful operation of railcars in the British Isles. No. 4 was built in 1934 and eventually went to the National Collection at York in 1979. Later there arrived at Didcot the more modern railcar No. 22, dating from 1940, which had been repainted into GWR livery on the Severn Valley Railway. It has been a regular performer at GWS open days for many years now and is as popular as any combination of steam locomotive and carriages. A rather more controversial arrival was 'Hymek' No. 7018. Built by Beyer Peacock in 1961 13 years after the demise of the GWR, it helped bring about the end of steam on the Western Region, along with the other two principal classes of diesel-hydraulics, the 'Warships' and the 'Westerns'. It was the last of its class

in service and was withdrawn in 1975 after a short but busy career. It is owned by the Diesel & Electric Group, which has put in thousands of hours restoring it to working order and repainting it in its original handsome livery of GWR green, pale green, light grey window surrounds, and yellow front-end. Its first main line outing for many years, though not under its own power, was to the Old Oak Common depot open day in September 1985.

Meanwhile, on the steam scene, more and more locomotives were arriving, some in working condition, while others were from Barry scrapyard, with years of restoration work ahead of them. Whether they were for service, or merely for static display, the GWS was also building up an unrivalled collection of GWR carriages. Like the locomotives, their condition varied enormously, from the practically perfect to the totally derelict. Some were fit only to provide parts for restorable

compatriots or for the Museum. Inevitably, those which have been restored to running order are the most modern vehicles, dating from the 1930s to the 1950s. Others came out of departmental service with BR and may have been 'gutted' internally, although mechanically, they were often in quite reasonable running condition.

In these early days carriage preservation and restoration came a very poor second to locomotives, both at Didcot and nationally, and when the Society did get to grips with the carriage scene it was soon realised that to put back into pristine condition a vehicle such as 'Dreadnought' No. 3299 which didn't look at all bad at first glance, was actually as big an undertaking as putting an ex-Barry inmate back into steam. For much of the 1970s the carriage department concentrated in keeping the Society's Vintage Train up to the high standards demanded by British Rail for main line running.

This aerial view of Didcot illustrates how the GWS Railway Centre is completely surrounded by busy BR main lines. The turntable, traverser, carriage and transfer sheds are visible beyond the main engine shed building. Taken in September 1982, the picture shows the original main line station building, since replaced. *Mike Esau.*

Although it was a sad day in some respects when it made its last main line run on January 26 1980, it did mean that the pressure was taken off the department in keeping ten carriages fit for main line service. There was now time to concentrate on some of the real GWR veterans which the Society had acquired in its early days, but which had only been partly restored. Two vehicles which especially deserve mention are No. 1941 an all-third non-corridor clerestory of 1901 and 'main line and city' non-corridor brake-third toplight No. 3755, of 1921.

Both are run-of-the-mill carriages, never used on the glamorous expresses or for anything out of the ordinary. In the early days of preservation it was the royal saloons or the Pullmans which attracted attention, and consequently there are plenty of this grand and glorious breed dotted around the country in preservation, but very few ordinary carriages survive, of the sort which were once so commonplace that no one gave them a second glance. In many ways these carriages are perhaps most worthy of all for preservation, precisely because they

are so ordinary, and thus so typical. It might be worth adding that restoration work on 1941 began some 20 years ago!

Wagon restoration is possibly the least publicised activity at Didcot, and this is a pity, for what was a steam railway without its enormous variety of wagons, which could be seen anywhere from great marshal-

Below: Unique Churchward 'Mogul' No. 5322, at Didcot in April 1981. This locomotive was completed in August 1917 at Swindon and sent immediately to France, for use with the British Army.
Michael H.C. Baker.

Top: Churchward '28XX' 2–8–0 No. 3822 at Barry scrapyard on November 2 1975, awaiting movement to Didcot, carried out in May 1976. The locomotive was built in April 1940 and withdrawn in January 1964. Following a full overhaul by a group of volunteers known at Didcot as 'the '38' mob,' the engine re-entered service in July 1985. No. 3822 is pictured at work on the demonstration line (above right) on September 28 1985. Fund raising activities for No. 3822 included the production of a series of T-shirts and sweat shirts (above) inscribed with a variety of slogans! *Graham Scott-Lowe/Peter Treloar/ GWS.*

ling yards, such as those in the big cities and at locations such as Severn Tunnel Junction, to the quiet siding at a wayside country station? There are still a few Great Western built wagons in service with BR, mostly on departmental duties, although steel is still conveyed from Poole to South Wales on GW 'flats' built during World War II. However the once-great variety of stock at work has inevitably lessened and the GWS now cares for the finest collection of both restored and unrestored GWR goods vehicles in Britain, some vehicles dating back to the 19th century. Their greatest 'moment of glory' came on July 28 1985, when 14 vehicles provided a nicely varied load for '28XX' 2–8–0 No. 3822, when she made her first public appearance in steam at Didcot fol-lowing restoration from scrapyard condition.

No enterprise, however splendid, is without its failures, and the GWR had its share. Some drawbacks, like Brunel's first engines, were apparent almost instantly and dealt with. But there were others which only became apparent long after they had come to be accepted as part of the Great Western way of doing things. The most heroic Great Western failure in this respect was the broad gauge. On the other hand, if failure can be said to be in the eye of the beholder, then there are still those who would claim that, like the proud mother watching her national serviceman son on his passing-out parade, it was everyone else who was out-of-step, then any charges of failure should be laid at the door of

Above: The lifting shop at Didcot, at the rear of the main shed, is the location for heavy overhauls on the GWS fleet. In this view, 'Hall' No. 5900 *Hinderton Hall* is being lifted for attention in 1976. *GWS.*

Left: the new steel front tubeplate fabricated and fitted during restoration of No. 3822. The tubeplate was made free of charge for the GWS by Durbin & Smith Ltd, of Widnes, Cheshire. *Nigel Harris.*

the other Companies for failing to appreciate the true value of the broad gauge system. Such hypothetical and insoluble arguments have kept many a historian in a very decent manner for a lifetime but the fact is that the last Broad Gauge train ran past Didcot on May 21 1892 and by the time the GWS had set up home there some 70 years later, no-one supposed that, whatever else was displayed, there would be much more of the broad gauge on show other than documents, a few photographs and the documented reminisences of long-dead Victorians.

However, it never does to close any chapter in the railway preservation story with too great a display of confidence. One can be fairly certain that while no original GWR broad gauge locomotive is going to turn up, there is a 7ft 0¼in gauge locomotive with GWR connections still in existence in the Azores, and sections of carriages and pieces of bridge rail in use as fencing had long been known about in various locations in the West Country. But it was a Taunton Group committee member with the splendidly Brunellian name of Amyas Crump who, in 1977, set in motion a GWS broad gauge restoration project which still continues, and which has become the centrepiece of a re-creation of the broad gauge on an infinitely greater scale than the founders of the Society could ever have envisaged.

Amyas reported to the Taunton Group that some distinctly ancient overgrown trackwork existed at the Burlescombe Yard of what had been the Westleigh Mineral Railway adjoining the West of England main line on the Somerset/Devon border. It was known that it was bridge rail, dating back well into broad gauge days, certainly to the 1870s and perhaps even earlier. What was then unknown was whether it existed in any quantity. Investigations by Taunton Group members as they cleared their way through the undergrowth through the Summer of 1978 revealed that there was far more rail than had ever been found anywhere else, and that it was in basically excellent condition, certainly good enough to carry trains for many more years — if it could be recovered. With the permission of the owners, ECC Quarries, the Group's finds were recorded, and on a winter morning in late 1978, before dawn, lifting began. It was a mammoth task for the eight-strong team, but by evening 750ft of rail, including four complete turnouts, parts and material for others, had been recovered. The weight of all this was 17½ tons. Most of it was put into store in Taunton, one turnout was donated to the National Railway Museum at York, and plans went ahead for the future of the remaining matcrial.

Inevitably, a very important component of the original broad gauge track, the woodwork, was missing, and several thousand pounds worth would have to be bought if the plans the Group had for relaying it at Didcot were to come to fruition. A great many fittings and small components were made up at the Taunton Depot. It would be tedious to list the vast number of jobs and operations which went on to gather together, make and assemble all the components needed before relaying could start. To the public — and to many GWS members too — the start proper was made in August 1980 when a working party of between 20 and 30 members descended on the north end of the Didcot site and began laying the longitudinal timber baulks upon which the ancient rails

Right (above): A peaceful winter's scene at Didcot Halt during the bitterly cold weather of early 1986. The Halt truly captures the spirit of the GWR with its 'pagoda' shelter, lower-quadrant signals, gas lamps, cast-iron notices and signal box. Who would have thought it possible in the corner of a locomotive shed yard? *Frank Dumbleton*.

Right (below): A sight to make any 'ganger' scratch his head! Mixed-gauge pointwork under construction outside the transfer shed at Didcot Railway Centre. Note the longitudinal timber baulks beneath the rails and the signals controlling operations on the branch. *Frank Dumbleton*.

would be laid. They toiled throughout the subsequent week and on Sunday August 31 an historic event took place when, to quote Taunton Group Secretary David Hartland: the Great Western Society operated "the first broad gauge train run since 1892 . . . and this occurred on the 145th anniversary of the incorporation of the GWR." The train may not have been terribly impressive, a hand-trolley in fact, rebuilt from parts recovered at Burlescombe and, since most broad gauge locomotives carried names from Greek mythology, the trolley is affectionately known today as *Phoebe*.

By September 27 1980 the first mixed broad and standard gauge (or narrow as the Taunton Group loftily insist on labelling the 4ft 8½in!) line to be opened since goodness-knows-when was ready. The replica *Rocket*, built for the Liverpool & Manchester Railway 150th anniversary celebrations earlier that year, was visiting Didcot and the following message flashed out on Paddington station's electronic departure board: "Mr Isambard Kingdom Brunel, Engineer of the Great Western Railway Company, magnanimously invites Mr. Robert Stephenson to demonstrate his new locomotive 'Rocket' on the mixed gauge lines at Didcot Railway Centre." Let David Hartland, who himself played the part of the great 'IKB' tell what happened.

"On Saturday morning Mr. Brunel and his followers waited patiently beside the 'transfer shed' as crowds gathered to observe this exciting spectacle. At the appointed hour (or somewhat behind it owing to problems of communication and differing railway time between the Northern Division and the rest of the site), Mr. Stephenson appeared, driving his locomotive steadily along the narrow gauge running line.

At this the whole assemblage was hushed. Mr. Brunel then proceeded to examine in the greatest of detail the trackwork, endeavouring to ascertain that it was safe for the passage of the locomotive. A murmur passed through the assembled company as Mr. Brunel gave the signal to proceed. Mr. Stephenson waved an acknowledgement and slowly the *Rocket* moved carefully and ceremoniously, backwards onto the baulk road. The silence was broken — the crowds cheered, cameras clicked and Mr Brunel stood back as *Rocket* swept past, with Mr. Stephenson valiantly attempting to reverse the motion of his locomotive before imminent collison with the transfer shed, (The 'Rocket' has most negligently not been provided with any form of brake appliance). Having arrested his progressive motion in time, Mr Stephenson stepped down to exchange salutations and hearty greetings with the broad gauge party."

The transfer shed, mentioned several times in David's account, is an integral, and most fortuitously so, part of the broad gauge scheme. It is one of the oldest Great Western artefacts still in existence, having been erected just west of Didcot station in 1856. Within it, transfer took place of goods from narrow to broad gauge wagons. Rather remarkably this ancient wooden building survived into the 1970s, and with the help of Manpower Services Commission schemes, the GWS dismantled it and re-erected it within the Railway Centre at the northernmost end of the site. The laying of broad gauge track in 1980 saw it restored to its original function, with the right-hand, and clearly wider arch over the mixed gauge track, the narrower, left-hand arch spanning the 'narrow gauge' metals.

Above: Railcars Nos.22 and 4 inside the shed at Didcot, stabled alongside No. 5900 *Hinderton Hall*. No. 22 remains at Didcot, while No. 4 is now on display at the GWR Museum, Swindon. *Michael H.C. Baker.*

Much remained to be done after the 1980 opening, and work has since proceeded steadily on further tracklaying, completion of the transfer shed itself, construction of a platelayers hut and the installation of a disc-and-crossbar signal. This is perfectly authentic in appearance and function, although it is made up from many parts including (whisper it softly!) a lamp from an LMS crossing gate. The Taunton Group wished to add to the display a signal box from the broad gauge period, and as the Bristol Group are the Society's signalling experts, in October 1984 its members brought Frome North box from its home of more than 100 years, from where it had controlled West of England, Weymouth and Radstock line trains since the broad gauge era. It will be some time before the box can be re-erected at Didcot but when this is done, Frome North box will revert to its original name of 'Frome Mineral Junction' and will in all respects be restored to its 1876 condition and appearance.

The culmination of the Taunton's Groups efforts will surely be realised when a genuine broad gauge steam locomotive steams up and down the baulk road. Although the Science Museum *Iron Duke* reproduction visited Didcot during the 1985 GW150 celebrations, it was not lifted off its narrow gauge (4ft 8½in!) carrying wagon. However, its stay during 1986 is likely to be much longer and before the year is out we will surely, for the first time since 1892, once again be treated to the

spectacle of a GWR designed broad gauge 'Single' steaming along Brunel's unique baulk road.

To the enthusiast practically every little bit of the railway scene is a delight, though the ordinary passenger may well see it quite differently. All he wants is to reach his destination with the least possible fuss, though what he takes for granted above all else is that on a train he will be safe. It wasn't always so in the early days and Brunel doesn't seem to have put signalling high on his list of priorities. Nevertheless, once the GWR got its priorities right then it was just about the safest railway in the world. Strictly speaking an enclosed private railway site such as Didcot doesn't need proper signals at all. However, if the story of the Great Western is to be properly and comprehensively told then the means by which, for example, long trundling coal trains and the 'Cheltenham Flyer' could

share the same tracks, and run to time, even in conditions of thick fog, could not be neglected by the Society's volunteers.

It was the Bristol Group of the CWS which took on this responsibility to tackle signalling. Plans were laid way back in the 1960s but it wasn't until the second running line, or the 'branch line' as it quickly became known, opened in 1981, that it all began to come together. In May 1972 the group removed the fittings from Radstock West when these became redundant, and in November 1975 the box itself was brought to Didcot. Much equipment had been gathered over the years from many other parts of the former GWR system. When the 'branch line' opened Radstock West box had been re-erected and was externally restored to pristine GWR condition. In its former existence it had controlled a level crossing. Many such crossings still exist, of course, but very few now possess the old type of hand-worked gates and those that remain surely cannot last much longer. A working crossing was obviously going to be a great attraction at Didcot. All the parts, rather like an enormous 'Airfix' assembly kit were stored at Didcot and in the three years from 1981 they were reassembled, so that for the great 1985 150th anniversary fortnight it was possible for visitors

Below: No. 4942 *Maindy Hall*, rescued from Barry scrapyard in 1973, alongside the Didcot coaling stage. The GWS has plans to convert this locomotive into a '29XX' series 'Saint' class 4–6–0, from which type the 'Hall' was originally derived. *Michael H.C. Baker.*

Left: The 'raw material' from which the Great Western Society's Carriage & Wagon Department members recreate the chocolate and cream splendour of the GWR's passenger stock, or the neatly lettered wagons of its good fleet. *GWS.*

Below: A superb example of the 'C&W' gang's efforts is the Travelling Post Office sorting van No. 814 (built 1940), which is also a very popular attraction at open days. The TPO is seen here collecting mail bags from the trackside equipment on the main Didcot demonstration line. *Mark Wilkins.*

to watch a steam-hauled goods or passenger train rumble over the crossing under the gaze of the signalman, who would then open the gates with the traditional wheel, and for them to then cross over the cobbles to the other side. It was amusing to watch the first performances of this latest Didcot experience. At first the pedestrians stood hesitantly after the gates opened, wondering if they really *ought* to cross, but once the first had dared, then like migrating birds they all flocked over! Truth to tell, having made the crossing there is little to do then but run round and come back, but this seems to be quite sufficient: the Society has been able to give its visitors an example of a fully operational, traditional gated level crossing.

Great thought has gone into the signals erected along the 'branch line'. As many varieties, from as many periods as possible, were obviously desirable, but they had to look authentic and function correctly. They had to be built because they were necessary, and not just set-up haphazardly, just for the sake of it. Apart from any other considerations, all signalling arrangements have to be examined and approved by the railway Inspectorate at the Department of Transport. The oldest signal we have produced is a disc-and-crossbar type of Brunel design, located beside the broad gauge track. Although totally authentic in appearance and operation, it is reconstructed from a number of separate parts, all such original signals having disappeared long ago. The 'branch' also has a number of the still familiar semaphores, some with wooden posts, with some metal posts and at least one concrete example. The connections, levers and trackside rodding are all authentic.

The second GWR signal box, from Frome North, was acquired and brought to Didcot in October 1984, and this will eventually be re-erected at the other end of the branch line, so that visitors to both boxes — there have already been thousands to Radstock West — will be able to see one box communicating with the other and watch how the safety of the passengers and goods was cared for, and how the responsibility for the safe running of trains passed

A tongue-in-cheek, though nonetheless stern warning on one of the carriage shed doors... *Nigel Harris.*

step-by-step, from box to box, from journeys beginning to end.

The GWR is affectionately recalled by many people for its glorious chocolate and cream stock, and the society's coaches are cared for in the carriage shed and workshop. Carriages, however beautifully restored, rapidly deteriorate if left out in the elements. In the early days a few were squeezed into the engine shed, but this was no sort of long-term solution, so in 1977 work began on a proper six-road carriage shed with a restoration bay and workshop. Outside is a traverser which is powered by a remarkable little vehicle, which was once steam-operated, then electrically driven, and presently powered by a Mini-Metro engine kindly donated by British Leyland. The traverser came from (once again, whisper it softly!) not Swindon Works but Derby. Similarly, the 70ft turntable is not of GWR origin but was built by Southern Railway, having been used

Above: The carriage shed traverser in action on March 8 1986, with 12-wheel special saloon No. 9002 (built 1940) on board: The vehicle has much restoration work ahead. *GWS.*

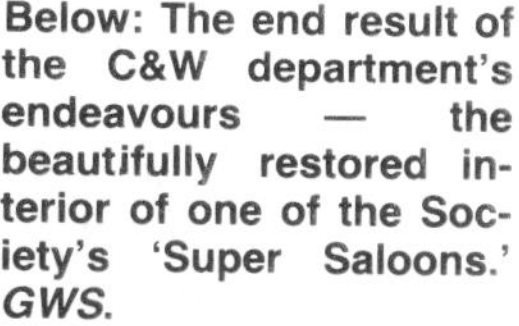

Below: The end result of the C&W department's endeavours — the beautifully restored interior of one of the Society's 'Super Saloons.' *GWS.*

Above: GWR 'Mink A' ventilated van No. 101720 (built 1924) in ex-works condition after restoration by the Great Western Society. A splendid vehicle, every bit as deserving of attention as the more glamorous prestige passenger stock. *GWS.*

by locomotives rostered for Ocean Liner expresses on Southampton Docks. When steam ceased on the Western Region, BR had removed the original GWR 65ft diameter turntable from Didcot and the Society had to widen and deepen the original pit when it obtained the larger Southampton structure which was put back into commission in the summer of 1978. The opening ceremony was performed appropriately by BBC Radio 2 'disc-jockey' David Hamilton, a man well-used to turntables; he is one of many celebrities who have come to Didcot over the years.

Finally the locomotive shed itself. Just inside on the left are the offices for the administration of the Centre, extensively rebuilt in the winter of 1985–6. Other offices and stores still serve their original purpose. Each shed road, approximately 200ft long, can take either three tender or up to six tank locomotives and they are numbered one to four from left to right. No. 1 road continues past the gentlemen's toilet, under wooden doors, and into the lifting shop. This might be said to be the heart of the GWS, for it is here that the heavy machinery, much of it installed by the Society, is located and on which so much of the restoration work is carried out. The electrically operated hoist can handle weights of up to 50 tons, and boilers needing repair or examination are separated from their frames here. All around are power tools, lathes and other equipment, including a lathe of considerable historic, although not railway, interest, for it was used in the building of Sir Frank Whittle's first jet engine. Visitors can always poke their noses in through the doorway and see what is going on, although for safety reasons it is not usually possible to let the public inside when work is in progress.

Above: The 'GWS 150' event, held at Didcot Railway Centre in May 1985 was an outstanding success for the Great Western Society, and visiting locomotives added much variety and interest. On May 25 1985, LNER 'A2' 'Pacific' No. 532 *Blue Peter*, from the Dinting Railway Centre, and '94XX' 0–6–0PT No. 9466, from the Buckinghamshire Railway Centre, are working on the main demonstration line at Didcot.

Right: No. 9466, seen here in its GW 150 guise as sister engine No. 9404, drifts into Didcot Halt on May 23 1985, during the Great Western Society's 'GWS 150' celebratory event. This Halt recaptures the classic atmosphere of the GWR branch station, once common all over the Company's system. *Both: Mick Roberts*

CHAPTER 4

CELEBRATING GREAT WESTERN 150

Charles Whetmath

EVEN before the Liverpool & Manchester Railway 150th anniversary was celebrated at Rainhill in 1980, the first steps had been taken to plan for GW150 in 1985. Those who know something of Great Western history will point out that the first section of the GWR was opened from Paddington to Maidenhead in 1838, so why celebrate in 1985? However, there was a precedent of sorts, for this merely followed the somewhat unorthodox decision of the GWR back in 1932 to commemorate its centenary on August 31 1935, 100 years after its Act of Incorporation received the Royal Assent. Consequently, the GWS called a meeting at Paddington in February 1980, which was attended by most of the GW-based preservation societies and various ideas were discussed. The Shildon and Rainhill events had featured a cavalcade of locomotives as their centrepieces, but at that time it was not known whether the Western Region would become involved in any GWR 150 celebrations. As time passed there was further spasmodic discussion, but little decision could be achieved until the Western Region announced in 1983 that it would indeed be marking the anniversary with a series of events, including a number of very special steam train operations together with a major exhibition at Swindon. However, unlike the previous anniversary events, the Swindon exhibition was planned as a basically static affair, as the site did not lend itself to an operating display.

Accordingly the GWS decided that it would organise its own special event at Didcot, with the accent on action. The layout and facilities at

A very nostalgic scene at Teignmouth as Didcot-based 'Castle' 4–6–0 No. 5051 *Drysllwyn Castle* and the SVR's 'Hall' 4–6–0 No. 4930 *Hagley Hall* sweep along the sea wall with the up 'Great Western Limited.' of July 14 1985. *Mark Wilkins.*

the shed lend themselves to this type of event as everything can be displayed and made accessible to visitors who can see what is going on around them, and with careful timetabling a constantly changing programme of operations provides maximum interest. The title 'Great Western Steam 150' was evolved to combine the Society's initials and emphasise the accent on action. The timing was also critical; it was realised that there would be little point in staging such a show to coincide with the Swindon exhibition, as that would probably be counter-productive and in any case most GW locomotives, including several from Didcot, would be away at Swindon. By early 1984 thoughts were turning to Spring Holiday and this idea received the blessing of the WR; a two-week event spread across the holiday would encompass school term in the first week, replacing the regular July Steamdays for Schools, and in the second week it would include the schools' half-term holiday, which is also a time when many people take a Spring break. The passage of time was to prove the wisdom of this choice, which was further aided by some of the best weather of the summer of 1985.

Meanwhile, lists were being prepared of locomotives that might be available to come to the exhibition. Informal discussion with a number of owners had already elicited considerable interest though one major railway dismissed the whole idea as an unworkable notion. Gradually a definitive list emerged but the inevitable happened as several locomotives dropped out for various reasons. One of the main concerns at this time, which took up a considerable amount of time at meetings of the Society's Council, was the funding of the event; various estimates of the likely attendance produced widely differing results and in any case much of the finance needed to bring locomotives would have to be available before the cash

Above: 'Castle' 4–6–0 No. 5051 *Drysllwyn Castle* and 7029 *Clun Castle* emerge from Parsons Tunnel to skirt the sea wall at Dawlish Warren with a single coach in tow, on September 9 1985, during movements connected with that month's GW 150 main line workings in the south west. *Peter J. C. Skelton.*

came in. A number of efforts were made to gain sponsorship but although some contributions were received there was no substantial response. However, by the autumn of 1984 it was becoming clear that there could be sufficient visiting engines at Didcot to justify a £4 per head admission price, and to encourage advance bookings this was reduced to £3 for postal bookings received by the end of April.

A big problem from the commercial view point was that although there would be an impressive variety of GWR engines for the enthusiasts that were none booked thus far with wide public appeal. The Science Museum's reproduction of the broad gauge *Iron Duke* would be attending for part of the event, but an agreement had been made that after its unveiling in Kensington Gardens, at Easter, it would not be seen again in steam

VISITING LOCOMOTIVES AT DIDCOT RAILWAY CENTRE 1985

Number, name and type:		From:	Period of loan & points of interest:
LNER No. 532 *Blue Peter*	4–6–2	Dinting Railway Centre	GWS150
GWR No. 813	0–6–0ST	Severn Valley Railway	GWS150. Ex-Port Talbot Railway
GWR No. 3217 *Earl of Berkeley*	4–4–0	Bluebell Railway	On loan 1984–1986
GWR No. 5224	2–8–0T	Great Central Railway	GWS150
GWR No. 6000 *King George V*	4–6–0	Bulmer Railway Centre, Hereford	1 September – 12 October
GWR No. 6619	0–6–2T	North Yorkshire Moors Railway	GWS150
LMS No. 8431	2–8–0	Keighley & Worth Valley Railway	GWS150 Built for LMS by GWR Swindon
GWR No. 9466 (also ran as 9404)	0–6–0PT	Quainton Railway Centre	GWS150, retained till October 1985
Nord No. 3.628	4–6–0	Nene Valley Railway	GWS150
GWR *Iron Duke*	4–2–2	Science Museum	GWS150 Broad gauge reproduction

A shed scene evocative of bygone years in atmosphere at least, as a cosmopolitan selection of motive power is steamed at Didcot for the GWS 150 event in May 1985. Locomotives on view include No. 5572, 0-6-2T No. 6619, LMS '8F' 2-8-0 No. 8431, LNER 'A2' No. 532 *Blue Peter* and Nord compound 4-6-0 No. 3.628. *Michael H.C. Baker.*

until the Swindon extravaganza in August, so it would not be as much of an attraction as it would have been in action on the Didcot broad gauge metals. Whilst it had been hoped to have a representative selection of non-GWR engines, the only one promised at this time was the Keighley & Worth Valley Railway's LMS Stanier 2–8–0 No. 8431, one of the batch built at Swindon during World War II, but then the Science Museum offered its French de Glehn 'Compound' 4–6–0 from the Nene Valley Railway. The Great Western connection here was the purchase back in 1903 of three de Glehn 'Atlantics' by Churchward, for comparative trials with his new standard locomotives, and the French 4–6–0 was a surprising omission from the Swindon exhibition list.

In January 1985 came the issue of a series of 'Famous Trains' postage stamps by the GPO, ostensibly to celebrate GW150 but only two of the five stamps featured Great Western Railway locomotives. All the stamps featured Terence Cuneo paintings and the artist was one of the guests aboard the Venice Simplon-Orient Express Pullman train which the GPO chartered to run from Paddington to Didcot to launch them onto the market. In the week prior to this event the BBC children's television programme 'Blue Peter' had descended on Didcot on a very

bleak, snowy day and it was decided to ask one of the programme's presenters, Simon Groom, to formally open GWS150. His agreement led in turn to a late decision to see if the LNER class A2 'Pacific' *Blue Peter* could come to Didcot for the event and thanks to its owner Geoff Drury, Dinting Railway Centre and British Railways, its move was organised at comparatively short notice. This engine was just what the Society was looking for to help make the event appeal to the general public as well as the enthusiast, despite it not being of Great Western origin.

Time was getting short and all the other arrangements were coming together but it was the co-ordination of the various locomotive movements that occupied most of the time of the Society's General Manager, Mick Dean. It is ironic that it was easier and cheaper to move most of the locomotives by road rather than rail. The only one that it was intended to move by rail, apart from *Iron Duke* which was loaded on two well-wagons, was No. 532 *Blue Peter* because of its size and the lack of suitable road access at Dinting, but early in May heavy rain in Yorkshire meant that it was impossible to load 2–8–0 No. 8431 onto a road trailer so there was further frenzied activity as another 'dead on own wheels' special rail freight move had to be arranged to haul No. 8431 to Dinting to join No.

532 *Blue Peter*, ready for award movement to Didcot.

GWS 150 opened on May 18 1985 and during the week beforehand the engines being brought by road were delivered to Milton Freight Terminal whence they were 'tripped' to the Didcot Railway Centre using the local 0–6–0 350hp diesel shunter. The de Glehn 'Compound' caused special problems because of its Continental width and height, but a route was successfully devised and it arrived on Friday May 17, in the company of '56XX' 0–6–2T No. 6619 and 2–8–0T No. 5224. The day was spent preparing for the opening.

Fortunately, the correct message was transmitted and the sun shone on God's Wonderful Railway on May 18. There were 11 engines in steam that day and for the next 15 days there were never less than five engines at work, despite some anxious moments over water supply and dubious coal quality in the aftermath of the miners' strike. Because it is only fitted with air brakes the French engine could only be used on freight trains, and saddle tank No. 813, with no continuous brake, was adopted as shed pilot, but all the other engines took their turn on passenger trains, either singly or in pairs, providing some highly unusual combinations. The visiting engines were normally operated by their own crews accompanied by a GWS pilotman, who was a qualified footplateman.

As the days passed it became clear that the whole event would be a success financially as well as operationally. The bombshell that Swindon Works was definitely to close in 1986 had exploded in the days preceding and there was considerable speculation as to how that would affect the planned August exhibition. We found out a couple of weeks later that the exhibition would be cancelled, although there had been hopes for a while of changing the venue and Didcot was one of a number of places considered. This presented a few problems as some of the exhibits had been going straight on to Swindon and new moves had to be considered. Pannier tank No. 9466 liked Didcot so much that it was October before it returned home to Quainton Railway Centre. As it turned out, GWS 150 was the one event of the year where the preservationists gathered to celebrate the anniversary, and although it was hard work, everyone enjoyed the experience.

The first main line operations as part of BR's GW150 celebrations to involve the Society took place at this time. BR assembled an Exhibition Train which did a grand tour of the former GWR system starting at Paddington in May and visiting GWS 150 for the last weekend of the event. It went on to Birmingham Moor Street on June 4 and the train was steam hauled by No. 5051 *Drysllwyn Castle* on this leg of its journey; on the previous Tuesday evening there was a test run to Oxford, the engine's first main line outing following a winter overhaul which included replacement of three cylinder linings.

Meanwhile, there was an Open Day at Reading Diesel Depot on June 1 and small 'Prairie' tank No. 5572 took a very unusual freight train comprising diesel railcar No. 22 and *Iron Duke* on its wagons. The cancellation of the Swindon exhibition had interrupted the programme of main line tours and at late notice No. 5051 travelled to Cardiff Canton Open Day on July 6 prior to joining No. 4930 *Hagley Hall* on their scheduled 'Great Western Limited' train from Bristol Temple Meads to Plymouth the following day. After the ignominious failure of both 4–6–0 No. 6000 *King George V* and 4–6–0 and No. 7819 *Hinton Manor* on the inaugural train on Easter Sunday, all eyes were on this train, but it too failed to reach Plymouth, the engines stalling on Dainton Bank due to a combination of very poor coal on 4–6–0 No. 4930 *Hagley Hall*, a track circuit failure at Aller Junction and greasy rails. The train terminated at Totnes after a diesel had propelled it up to Dainton Summit and the engines finally reached Laira Depot very late that night. Because of these problems it was decided that the up train the following Sunday would start from Newton Abbot to avoid the South Devon banks and this trip passed uneventfully.

Despite the cancellation of the Swindon exhibition it was decided to go ahead with the ambitions programme of steam trains that had been arranged between Swindon and Gloucester during August. As British Rail Engineering staff refused to have anything to do with GW 150, the turntable and other facilities at Swindon Works were unavailable so the engines had to be based at Gloucester Horton Road shed, being towed tender-first to and fro at the beginning and end of each day. No. 5051 took the inaugural train on Tuesday August 6 and it was booked to work another four trains, but unfortunately problems with a persistent steam leak caused No. 4930 to be substituted on August 13. This leak had been evident since its overhaul but the repairs effected at Gloucester finally cured the problem and the engine was at last able to demonstrate its true ability. Another casualty was the failure to complete the restoration of No. 6998 *Burton Agnes Hall*, so it was unable to take its turn on the Gloucester operations. All in all however, these trains were an outstanding success and with wonderful co-operation from the train crews some spirited runs were made. Not least was the boost to the Church Fund at Frampton Mansell where many enthusiasts congregated to photograph the trains on the climb to Sapperton Tunnel.

September saw more trains in the West Country, but BR abandoned further attempts to run steam into Plymouth, so the early morning of Sunday September 1 saw No. 5051 *Drysllwyn Castle* and No. 7029 *Clun Castle* heading west with one saloon to work a Plymouth-Bristol train that afternoon. They returned to Plymouth that night in readiness for No. 7029's trip to Truro on September 6, substituting for 4–4–0 No. 3440 *City of Truro*, Laira Deport Open Day on September 7 and another up train on Sunday September 8. There was a very complicated exhcange of engines during the month as No. 6000 *King George V* went to Didcot after working the last Gloucester-Swindon journey on September 1. On September 15 it worked with No. 5572 and 'Hymek' diesel No. D7018 from Didcot to the Old Oak Common Open Day.

Meanwhile, on the previous day No. 5051 *Drysllwyn Castle* worked the GWS 'Red Dragon' railtour from Swindon to Hereford via Gloucester and Newport, en route to Landore Depot Open Day. No. 5051 has the distinction of having been shedded at Landore for a quarter of a century from its construction at Swindon in 1936, and its return there was specially requested and caused a great deal of excitement. In conjunction with this there were three steam excursions each day between Swansea and Carmarthen on September 21/22, most being worked by No. 6960 *Raveningham Hall* but No. 5051 took the final journeys on Sunday afternoon. It then returned to Hereford, taking part in Open Days at the Bulmer Railway Centre whilst No. 6000 *King George V* appeared at Didcot's Enthusiasts' Weekend. Finally on October 12 the GWS ran another 'Red Dragon' railtour, this time with double steam working; No.6000 *King George V* took the train from Swindon to Hereford with No.5051 *Drysllwyn Castle* on the return trip.

That was the conclusion of GW150 as far as the Great Western Society was concerned although there were still some other events including a much-criticised 'mystery tour' to mark the return to steam after twenty five years of No.3440 *City of Truro*. The events of the year took a great deal of time to plan and organise, and many people spent a lot of holiday travelling around with No. 5051 to service it. but the enthusiasm and publicity generated, which could be measured in financial terms by the extra people who paid to come and visit Didcot Railway Centre, made it all worth while. So far as the GWS was concerned, GW150 was a success.

Above: A superb night-study of Riddles '9F' 2–10–0 No. 92220 *Evening Star*, standing outside the shed at Didcot on August 16 1980. The last steam locomotive to be built for British Railways, No. 92220 emerged from Swindon, trimmed with a copper-capped chimney, in 1960. *Richard Brown.*

CHAPTER 5

VISITORS

Michael H.C. Baker

SINCE the setting up of Didcot Railway Centre and its opening to the public in 1969 visitors of all shapes, sizes and capacities, ages and origins have appeared. There have also been many guest loco-motives. It is perhaps inaccurate to describe No. 4079 *Pendennis Castle* as a visitor, for this locomotive arrived at Didcot early in 1967 and did not leave until June 1972. In that time the 4–6–0 was only rarely in steam and its departure was not entirely amicable. But that is history and the 'Castle' certainly looked very fine, the first really big engine seen at Didcot in pristine GWR livery for some 20 years. Tyseley's double-chimney BR-built 'Castle', No. 7029, *Clun Castle* has been to Didcot on a number of occasions and its partner-ship both within the Centre pre-

cincts and out on the main line in 1985 with Didcot-based, No. 5051 *Drysllwyn Castle* has produced some stirring spectacles of sight and sound. Equally welcome has been the 'King', No. 6000 *King George V* although we may shortly be referring to 'the other King', for Quainton's No. 6024 *King Edward I* is nearing the end of his long restoration and hopefully may be seen at Didcot at some stage.

Three of the Severn Valley Railway's extensive collection of locomotives have appeared at Didcot. One was '4MT' Ivatt 2–6–0 No. 43106 which spent a wet afternoon with us in September 1980, having substituted for another LMS locomotive, 'Jubilee' 4–6–0 No. 5593 *Kolhapur* on a railtour from Birmingham, and reappeared on

another railtour the following April. Four years later a 'Jubilee' 4–6–0 did get to Didcot when No. 5690 *Leander*, from Bridgnorth, stayed for a month in between rostered mainline tours. The only Severn Valley-based GWR locomotive to visit us has been Port Talbot 0–6–0 saddle tank No. 813, in 1985.

Apart from *Pendennis Castle*, the two longest stays by visiting engines have been by Bulleid 'Pacific' No. 34051 *Winston Churchill* and '9F' 2–10–0 No. 92220 *Evening Star*, both from the National Collection. The 'Pacific' was never steamed but the Swindon built 2–10–0 really earned its keep. After appearing at Rainhill in 1980 the '9F' worked south and proved an enormous draw whenever it was steamed by the GWS. In November of that year No. 92220 hauled the 'Zenith' railtour as far as Birmingham and back (the 'King' had charge of the Shrewsbury — Chester section), the locomotive was retubed in 1981 and then went off to Stratford-on-Avon. The locomotive shared with *Drysllwyn Castle* the Old Oak 'shuttle', which ran between Paddington and Old Oak Common on September 20 1981 as part of the 75th anniversary celebrations of the depot, it then took part in 'Welsh Marches Pullman' workings, and after being steamed many times on No. 8 road No. 92220 went back to York in the spring of 1983.

David Shepherd's '9F' No. 92203 *Black Prince* called in at Didcot on its way to work the 'Royal Giants Tour' to Hereford in May 1973, whilst a third 2–10–0 was the big blue 'Austerity' *Gordon*, on its way to take up residence at Bridgnorth, in September 1971.

Four LNER locomotives have appeared at Didcot over the years 'A2' 'Pacific' No. 532 *Blue Peter* spent some time in the early '70s at Didcot without being steamed, whilst No. 4998, *Sir Nigel Gresley* the streamlined 'A4', and 'V2' 2–6–2 No. 4771 *Green Arrow* both came in on railtours on July 1 1973, to be followed by arguably the most famous steam locomotive of all 'A3' No. 4472 *Flying Scotsman* in October 1973. These were not the first LNER express locomotives seen at Didcot, although possibly they were the first to actually enter the shed. During World War II almost anything might have passed by, but even before this Great Northern and Great Central 'Atlantics', 'B17s' and other classes had a regular working between Swindon and Nottingham on the through Penzance — Newcastle express. One of the not normally particularly speedy Gresley 4–6–0s, No. 2863 *Everton* was so taken with the racing stretch west of Didcot that it actually beat the 'Cheltenham Flyer' schedule from Swindon to Steventon!

From the Southern, apart from No. 34051 *Winston Churchill* there has been one of the famous 'Terriers', No. 32670, which did an exchange with Collett 0–4–2T No. 1466, the

Right (above): The Severn Valley Railway's Ivatt '4MT' 2–6–0 No. 43106 is serviced at Didcot on September 27 1980, during main line railtour duties.

Right (below): BR-built 'Castle' 4–6–0 No. 7029 *Clun Castle* takes water at Didcot on April 16 1978, flanked by the National Railway Museum's Bulleid 'Pacific' No. 34051 *Winston Churchill*. Both: John Titlow.

The GWS vintage train made many journeys on Western Region metals until its withdrawal from main line service in January 1980. During a visit to the south west the train visited the Torbay & Dartmouth Railway on May 12 1979, when the train was hauled from Kingswear to Paignton in dramatic fashion by '4200' class 2–8–0T No. 5239. This picture was taken at Noss, near Kingswear. *Mark Wilkins*.

Above: The National Railway Museum's *Rocket* replica stands on the mixed gauge trackwork in front of the transfer shed at the northern end of the site on September 28 1980. *Richard Brown*.

Above: LNER ambassadors at Didcot on July 1 1973 were 'A4' No. 4498 *Sir Nigel Gresley* and 'V2' 2-6-2 No. 4771 *Green Arrow*. *Michael H.C. Baker*.

Left: 0–4–2T *Lion* — alias *The Titfield Thunderbolt* — ambles along the Didcot Railway Centre branch line, towards Didcot Halt, on October 10 1981. Built in 1838 *Lion* is the oldest standard gauge engine maintained in working order in Britain. *Peter Treloar*.

Left, top: No. 6000 *King George V* is the focus of attention at Didcot in sunny weather during its visit on July 3 1983. A 'royal' visit of this kind has much public appeal.

Left, below: Didcot Railway Centre-based 'Hymek' diesel hydraulic No. D 7018 stands in the diesel depot at Old Oak Common, during the BR open day in September 1985. *Both: Peter Treloar.*

it must have come regularly to Didcot. A bit of a tenuous link, perhaps; nevertheless the complete No. 3217 arrived at Didcot in the summer of 1984 for a two-year stay.

Like it or not, the GWR was instrumental in establishing the diesel locomotive as an acceptable motive power unit for both main and branch line use in this country and the Didcot Railway Centre would be neglecting a vital part of the Great Western story if it failed to take this fact into account. GWR railcar No. 4 spent many years with us before going on to the National Railway Museum for restoration and then to Swindon Museum. In the early days of the Society, BR sent along a variety of diesels to take part in Didcot open days, including the unique hydraulic transmission 'Westerns', 'Warships' and 'Hymeks'. No. 7018, of the 'Hymek' class, and owned by the Diesel & Hydraulic Group, was eventually to take up residence at Didcot and there have been proposals for a 'Western' to visit us, but this has not yet happened. The most unusual diesel motive power on a railtour to Didcot was a pair of English Electric Class 20s, both in the old green livery, which arrived from Derby in September 1979. Lately, much interest has been aroused by the many Class 58s, some with their first coat of paint barely dry, which work the Merry-Go-Round coal trains to the great power station whose chimneys and cooling towers so dominate Didcot and provide as significant a landmark as the prehistoric white horse carved into the chalk downs at Uffington overlooking the Didcot to Swindon main line.

The GWS has been pleased over the years to host visits by locomotives from other sites around the country, and we hope many more similar events of interest will follow in the years to come.

latter going off to the Kent & East Sussex Railway in the Spring of 1984. No. 32670 was built at the LBSCR's Brighton works in 1872 and ranks as the oldest main line locomotive to have been seen at Didcot in the GWS's 25 years. Another locomotive from Southern territory, although pure Great Western in origin, is 4–4–0 No. 3217 *Earl of Berkeley.* This delightful little engine was preserved by Mr.T.R. Gomm in 1962, to whom Great Western enthusiasts owe a great deal, for otherwise the sole surviving example of the many varieties of Swindon built double-framed 4–4–0, would be No. 3440 *City of Truro.* No. 3217 arrived in working order on the Bluebell Railway on February 15 1962 and has been a resident in Sussex ever since. The 'Earls' were long familiar at Didcot in GWR days, working down the Newbury and Winchester line, although No. 3217 herself was always a Cambrian-based engine. However its boiler and cab came from 'Duke' No. 3282 (her chassis was from 'Bulldog' No. 3425), and the engine was shedded at Oxford immediately before withdrawal, and

CHAPTER 6

OUT ON THE MAIN LINE
Michael H.C. Baker

Above: A beautiful recreation of the GWR on the main line by the Great Western Society. In a scene highly evocative of the pre-Nationalisation era, 'Manor' 4–6–0 No. 7808 *Cookham Manor* and 'Hall' 4–6–0 No. 5900 *Hinderton Hall* steam past Aynho Junction with 'The Capital Venturer' of October 6 1979.
Peter J. C. Skelton.

Right: On July 7 1985, Didcot-based 'Castle' 4–6–0 No. 5051 *Drysllwyn Castle* leads the Severn Valley Railway's 'Hall' 4–6–0 No. 4930 *Hagley Hall* away from Newton Abbot, bound for Plymouth, with 'The Great Western Limited' GW 150 special. This train stalled on Dainton Bank, due to a combination of poor coal, a track circuiting problem and greasy rails. *Hugh Ballantyne*.

No. 6998 *Burton Agnes Hall* gets away from Leamington on September 29 1973, with 'The William Shakespeare,' comprised of seven BR MK 1 vehicles and a pair of GWS restored carriages behind the tender.

ONE of the most recurring and powerful images in English writing concerns a grassy bank, high summer, and the thousand-and-one images evoked by the sounds, scents and colours of the English sky and countryside. It is a device which served the young William Shakespeare well, as it did William Blake, Jane Austen, Lewis Carroll and P.G. Wodehouse. Anyone who has ever sat beside a railway line to watch the passing of a particular train must surely have experienced what I am trying to describe; daydreaming as the sun beats down, with thoughts and fancies drifting as though with a will of their own.

I remember one such June afternoon at the GWR's Aynho Junction 25 years ago. Northamptonshire is not a county one normally associates with the Great Western Railway but nevertheless this is where Aynho belongs although the line immediately to the north and south is in Oxfordshire. It was a Saturday and the only diesel traction I had so far seen had been the DMU I had travelled in from Paddington; it was rather a novelty at the time. A succession of steam-hauled expresses had passed me by. Few 'stoppers' were ever needed in that lush rural north Chiltern countryside and there were no daytime paths for freight trains on a busy summer Saturday. The motive power ranged from 'King' 4–6–0s to 2–6–2Ts, but I was chiefly on the lookout for a Churchward 'Mogul'. One could always reckon on several of these elderly but still spritely maids-of-all-work appearing on top link duties on such a day. In the event there were Kings', 'Castles', 'Halls' and 'Granges' in profusion but as yet, no 2–6–0. The sun grew hotter, the bees buzzed, the grasshoppers 'chirruped', and I leaned back on the fence post at the top of the cutting, my thoughts distantly removed from railway matters. I therefore missed the lowering of the down distant, and before I could gather my wits a '53XX' 2–6–0 had burst under the flyover and was away chattering delightedly to itself over the rail joints and the junction as it bustled its 10 Collett and Stanier corridors towards Birmingham.

With some annoyance I watched the last bow-ender disappear from view but I was at least ready for the next up train, the Birkenhead–Brighton and Hastings express. It hove into view, on time, in charge of No. 7808 *Cookham Manor*. Such a locomotive would have been fairly unusual on such a duty during the week but it was far from remarkable on a summer Saturday. Remember, this was 1961 and although steam seemed to have a virtual monopoly on that particular day, its end had in fact been announced some years earlier. 1962 saw the 'Western' diesel-hydraulics wiping out the 'Kings' from their 34-year monopoly on the Paddington–Birmingham route, and steam would vanish for ever from the line, and everywhere else on the WR, within four years. Or so we thought.

Instead, through the enthusiasm of the preservation movement and the co-operation of British Rail it has still been possible through the 1970s and 80s to doze in the sun, and shiver in mid-winter too, beside Aynho Junction and watch *Cookham Manor, King George V,* a trio of 'Castles' and two 'Halls' and many other steam engines pass by

Right: On July 15 1973, the Dart Valley Railway's '14XX' 0-4-2T No. 1450 worked the Marlow branch to celebrate the centenary of 'the Marlow Donkey.' The locomotive and its two-coach GWS train are seen here amidst the small vessels of the Thames at Bourne End. *J.G. Mallinson.*

occasionally on their way to and from William Shakespeare's home town, whence odes about wild thyme and grassy banks no doubt still issue forth.

After No. 6000 *King George V* had broken the ban on main line steam running in 1971, it was lifted nationwide on the second weekend of June 1972 and No. 7029 *Clun Castle* headed a railtour to Didcot, passing Aynho Junction en-route, just as *King George V* had done the previous Autumn. The Great Western Society sent out its inaugural train on October 1 1972 behind No. 6998 *Burton Agnes Hall*. It was one of those Autumn days which seemed to have forgotten that summer was supposed to have made off weeks earlier, and although I watched No. 6998 and her 11 'corridors' pass through the green fields north of Didcot there were many observers in my old haunt at Aynho relishing the spectacle of a Swindon two-cylinder 4–6–0 speed under the flyover there for the first time in seven years since No. 6998 itself had passed for the last time on January 3 1966.

Over the years since 1971, four locomotives based permanently at Didcot have shared the main line railtour workings, although there have been many others which have either been resident at the depot for long or short stays which have had charge of railtours, and other Didcot locomotives which have gone out on the main line to take part in open days, film-making, or trials. For example in October 1974 No. 7808 *Cookham Manor* joined No. 6998 *Burton Agnes Hall*, the pair working to and from Tyseley and Stratford-on-Avon. The next year they went to Worcester and Hereford. On May 15 1976 No. 5900 *Hinderton Hall*, the first Didcot locomotive to be rescued from Barry scrapyard and restored to main line running condition, went to Birmingham with No. 6998. There were various other runs by the two-cylinder engines before January

An expertly panned shot of No. 1466 at work with its auto-train on the Wallingford branch, during a memorable day of operations on April 15 1968. *Brian Stephenson.*

1980, when No. 5051 *Drysllwyn Castle* appeared, just in time to make two runs to Stratford-on-Avon before the GWS Vintage Train was taken out of main line service.

The final run of the GWS main line stock on January 26 1980, a gloriously sunny, crisp day, represented for many the epitome of all that the Great Western Society had been striving for; ten chocolate and cream liveried GWR cariages in the charge of a Swindon-built four-cylinder express engine.

The vintage train's origins had coincided with the first appearance of the restored *Burton Agnes Hall* on

Above: 'Manor' 4–6–0 No. 7808 *Cookham Manor* and 'Hall' No. 6998 *Burton Agnes Hall* lead the GWS vintage train through delightful countryside near Great Malvern with an excursion working of June 14 1975.
G. Roy Hounsell.

Left: No. 7808 *Cookham Manor* pauses for breath beneath the sweeping arched roof at York station on August 11 1975, en-route to the Shildon celebrations held that year. Sights like this are a source of considerable pride for the GWS. *GWS Collection.*

the main line eight years before. On that original trip to Tyseley in October 1972 two GWR carriages went out with No. 6998. These were excursion-third No. 1289 (of 1937) and corridor-third No. 5952 (of 1935). To many the familiar chocolate and cream livery, the distinctive art-deco interior of No. 1289 and the age-old layout of a separate door to each compartment of No. 5952 were as welcome and attractive as the gleaming Brunswick green, copper-capped 4–6–0 at the front end.

Gradually, more Didcot carriages were passed for main line running. A good deal of the time they were hauled by diesels which produced some intriguing combinations. In May 1974 No. 1289 ventured out with a rake of blue and grey BR MK.1's is to Aberystwyth, where it met up with other GWR-built carriages on the narrow gauge Vale of Rheidol line. Three months later five GWS coaches went to Marylebone. They were needed for the filming of 'One of our Dinosaurs is Missing'. This marked the one and only time 'Mogul' No. 5322 has ventured on to the main line since arriving at Didcot earlier that year after restoration in South Wales. Although in the film the 2–6–0 gave every appearance of being in steam, in reality two small gas-fired boilers produced the convincing effects. No. 5322 was however acting as the genuine article a month later when she worked some of the vintage train vehicles on No. 8 road at the Enthusiasts Day. She was actually scheduled to take charge of a main line railtour but various defects made this impossible and the 2–6–0 has not steamed for more than ten years now. Many hope that this, one of the oldest and most distinctive locomotives of the Didcot collection, will soon be at work again. There are, after all, any manner of GWR 4–6–0s, 2–6–2Ts and pannier tanks in steam around the rail centres and branch lines, but

there is only one Churchward 2–6–0 left in the world.

In October 1974 sufficient carriages had been restored and declared fit for main line running for a complete GWS vintage train to take to the tracks. Seven vehicles, including the magnificent 'Ocean Saloon' No. 9118 *Princess Elizabeth*, of 1932, which provided the refreshments, made their stately way to Tyseley and Stratford-on-Avon behind the 'Manor' and the 'Modified Hall'. Didcot has three 'Ocean Saloons' and to travel in one of them, behind a steam engine,

represents just about the ultimate in dignifed, luxurious, nostalgic rail travel. They are to all intents and purposed identical in appearance and style, certainly externally, to the 1935 'Cornish Riviera' stock, and although only one example of this, a restaurant car on the Gloucestershire and Warwick Railway, has been preserved, the 'Ocean Saloons' when coupled together provide a cameo of how the 'Centenary Riviera' must have appeared. Was there, I wonder, ever a colour photograph taken of the Cornish Riviera in the late 1930s? 'Ocean Saloon' No. 9112 *Queen Mary* brought the Society's vintage train up to eight carriages.

September 1975 saw the vintage train carriages and a GWR locomotive venture yet further afield. To celebrate the 150th Anniversary of the Stockton & Darlington Railway No. 7808 *Cookham Manor* took four carriages and 'Siphon G' No. 2796 to the heart of North Eastern territory. Exhibit No. 48, to quote the official guide to the Shildon Cavalcade, was "the light-weight, modern, two-cylinder passenger locomotive *Cookham Manor*, whilst the presence was also recorded of our 'finely restored train'". Shildon marked the 'Siphon G's' first public appearance. The GWR's Siphon vans have a long, complex and intriguing history and the 'Gs' were the best known of the breed. They were ventilated bogie vehicles and were officially built to

46

Above: GWR 'Ocean' saloon *Princess Elizabeth* (built 1932) with the vintage train at Paddington, July 6 1978. *John Titlow.*

carry milk churns of which many thousand were brought each day from the West of England, Wales and the West Midlands to London, Bristol, Birmingham and other centres. As more and more milk went into tankers and then, sadly but only recently, on to the road, the 'Siphons' became general utility vehicles for parcels, pigeons, picnic hampers and just about anything that couldn't be trusted on a seat but was in a hurry and needed to be sent by fast van or passenger train. Didcot's No. 2796 was built in 1937. BR liked the design sufficiently for examples of 'Siphon Gs' to be built into the 1950s. In their latter days they were used for newspaper traffic and regularly worked down through Didcot on the night trains to the West, although others could be found far away on the Great Eastern section. The last was not withdrawn until 1983, several being broken up in the BR sidings at Didcot, but a few may still be found around the BR system in departmental service.

The final carriages to join the vintage train were the newest built vehicles. They were both of British Railways manufacture, though of GWR design. They were of the final bow-ended, sloping roof variety, reminiscent of LNER practice, but with the addition of inelegant slab sides, although internally they were very modern and forward-looking. No. 2202 was a brake third, built in 1950, and had not carried GWR livery until preservation, but No. 7372 was a rather special carriage. A brake composite built at the end of 1948, it had uniquely worn nothing but chocolate and cream having gone straight into the Western Region Royal Train.

The two 'Ocean Saloons' had to be left behind when we broke yet more new ground in April 1979, for their overall dimensions were too great — shades of Brunel's Broad Gauge — to permit them to run behind an LNER designed EM1 electric locomotive between Sheffield, Dinting, and Manchester Piccadilly. In March of that year the GWS was delighted to be invited by British Rail to break the 14-year steam ban at Paddington when at dawn No. 5900 *Hinderton Hall* steamed into the station, admittedly propelled by a diesel, with two GWR carriages, and spent the day there as the focus of much admiration, to celebrate the 125th anniversary of the Great Western's London terminus.

With time running out for the vintage train, the pace quickened through 1979. Two West of England visits saw the train running behind varied motive power. On the Torbay Railway the big eight-coupled tank No. 5239 had charge between Paignton and Kingswear, whilst a Class 33 diesel brought chocolate and cream carriages back to the Weymouth Harbour line when on July 8 1979 the original GWR route of the Channel Islands Express was followed by way of Castle Cary, Yeovil and Dorchester.

No less than four steam

MAIN LINE ACTIVITIES AND VISITS BY DIDCOT BASED LOCOMOTIVES: 1985		
No. 5051 *Drysllwyn Castle*	June	4 Exhibition Train Didcot–Birmingham Moor Street
	July	6 Cardiff Canton Open Day
		7 'Great Western Limited', Bristol Temple Meads–Totnes
		14 'Great Western Limited', Newton Abbot–Bristol Temple Meads
	August	6 Swindon–Gloucester and return
		11 Swindon–Gloucester and return
		18 Swindon–Gloucester and return
	Sept	1 'Great Western Limited', Plymouth–Bristol Temple Meads
		7 Plymouth Laira Open Day
		8 Great Western Limited Plymouth–Bristol Temple Meads
		14 'Red Dragon', Swindon–Hereford
		20 Neath Station Display
		21 Swansea Landore Open Day
		22 'Red Dragon', Swansea–Carmarthen and return
		28–29 Bulmer Railway Centre open weekend
	Oct	12 'Red Dragon', Hereford–Swindon
No. 5572	June	1 Reading Depot Open Day
	Sept	15 Old Oak Common Open Day
No. D7018		Sept 15 Old Oak Common Open Day
Diesel railcar No. 22	June	1 Reading Depot Open Day

Left: Representing the Great Western Society at the 150th anniversary celebrations of the Liverpool & Manchester Railway, in 1980, was 4–6–0 No. 5051 *Drysllwyn Castle* and a pair of the SVR's restored GWR carriages. This impressive ensemble is pictured passing the grandstand at Rainhill on May 25 1980. *R.J. Blenkinsop*

Below: No. 5051 *Drysllwyn Castle* has become the main line 'flagship' of the GWS since 1980 — especially during the GW 150 events of 1985. The 4–6–0 is seen here beating a path from Swansea with the final run of the day to Carmarthen on Sunday September 22, during a weekend of shuttle operations, handled principally by the SVR's 4–6–0 No. 6960 *Raveningham Hall*. *Peter J. C. Skelton*.

locomotives had charge of the ten carriages on two visits to the Severn Valley Railway in September and October 1979; No.7812 *Erlestoke Manor* and No. 7819 *Hinton Manor* on the first occasion and No. 4930 *Hagley Hall* and LMS Class 5 4–6–0 No 5000 on the second visit. The coming together of the ten GWR carriages from Didcot and the Severn Valley's splendid assortment of chocolate and cream beauties produced a mouth-watering plethora of Swindon-designed vehicles in original livery such as had not been seen since 1948 and, sadly, is not likely to be seen again.

One of the aspects which got neglected in all the excitement of seeing how many bits of the old Swindon empire could be covered by steam engines in 1985 was carriages. Although Didcot was getting on with some high quality restoration work throughout the year not one GWS carriage ventured out on the main line, and there was just one main line run each by vehicles from the Severn Valley Railway and the Birmingham Railway Museum.

Certainly, BR did its best with its rake of MK 1 vehicles repainted in chocolate and cream livery, and the SLOA Pullman rake made a splendid sight, but neither pretended to be the 'real thing'. When one considers that marvellous collection of vintage restaurant cars which toured the BR network to celebrate the centenary of rail catering in 1979 one wonders why a similar rake of genuine GWR carriages could not have been got together for main line operation during 1985.

To return to the vintage train, however, October 6 1979 was its one and only run behind the Great Western's pride and joy No. 6000 *King George V* when the 4–6–0 hauled the train from Shrewsbury to Hereford and Didcot. Strictly speaking December 31 was the deadline for the end of the vintage train's adventures on the main line. New regulations by BR meant that it was now beyond the resources of the GWS's band of volunteers to keep the carriages up to main line standards, added to which was the increasing backlog of restoration work on the many, older carriages and wagons at Didcot which were being neglected in order to keep the ten vintage train vehicles at work. However the long restoration from

Barry scrapyard condition to main line standards of 4–6–0 No. 5051 *Drysllwyn Castle/Earl Bathurst* was virtually complete as 1980 dawned and so special dispensation was given to run two final trips in January to Stratford-on-Avon behind the 'Castle'. There was not time to complete the 'Castle's' paintwork or lining out and so No. 5051 went out in austerity World War II condition, but still looked magnificent in charge of her train of ten chocolate and cream carriages, and on the final run on January 26 1980 was featured on BBC TV's national news.

The end of the Vintage Train main line operation was certainly the end of a splendid chapter in the Great Western Society's story, but it coincided with the opening of

Right: With whistles screaming, Nos. 5051 *Drysllwyn Castle* and 7029 *Clun Castle* roar through Tiverton Junction on the climb to Whiteball Summit with the 'Great Western Limited' of Sunday September 1 1985. This was the first time that a pair of 'Castles' had hauled a main line train in more than two decades. *Mark Wilkins.*

Below: 'Prairie' tank No. 5572 made a totally unexpected main line appearance when it ran under its own power to the Reading Open Day of June 1 1985, hauling the *Iron Duke* reproduction and GWR railcar No. 22. The ensemble is seen here working back to Didcot at Basildon, June 2 1985. *John Titlow.*

another one. No. 5051, which despite the inability of anyone east of Severn Tunnel Junction to pronounce its name has always been known as *Drysllwyn Castle* rather than *Earl Bathurst*, has become the most travelled of all Didcot's locomotives. She has gone north to Rainhill and met No. 673 *Maude* from the North British Railway, travelled west to Swansea, where in GWR and BR days she was long shedded at Llandore, and gone south-west to Plymouth and east to Paddington.

The GW Society has been in existence long enough for a number of its locomotives to have been through several cycles of work, rest, overhaul and work again. There are those, such as *Drysllwyn Castle*, which have been restored from scrapyard condition, and others which came straight from service with British Railways. Of the latter both *Cookham Manor* and *Burton Agnes Hall* eventually needed heavy repair work. Repairs on the 'Hall' were completed ready for the 1986

season. Then there are the Society's first two locomotives, tank engines Nos 1466 and 6106, both having been seen on the main line. No. 1466 reappeared from overhaul in 1981 and on September 7 1983 had the honour of conveying the retiring Chairman of British Rail, Sir Peter Parker, from Didcot mainline station to the Railway Centre for his farewell reception and celebrations. No. 6106 shared with No. 6998 *Burton Agnes Hall* the working of a steam shuttle service between Maidenhead and Bourne End on July 15 1974 as part of the Marlow branch centenary celebrations. Six years earlier No. 1466 and its auto-trailer No. 231 broke the BR steam ban by taking over the Wallingford branch at Easter 1968 and again in the following September, but unfortunately the powers-that-be stepped in to prevent a recurrence and subsequent special workings in association with Wallingford Carnival were formed of a BR DMU, although GWS members helped to run the show.

During 1985 Didcot returned two former Barry locomotives to steam, Collett 2–8–0 No.3822 and small 2–6–2T No. 5572. The former has yet to venture beyond the confines of the Centre but the tank engine sprang a considerable surprise when she went out unescorted to Reading Depot Open Day with diesel railcar No. 22 and the *Iron Duke* reproduction. She came back next morning, No. 5572 in charge of her highly unusual train proceeding down the main line as though Bristol at the very least was her objective.

Finally No. 5572 was off again, with *King George V* and the Diesel & Electric Group's 'Hymek', to the Old Oak Common Open day. This was a splendid extravaganza, with five engines in steam and many unusual diesels, operational and preserved on display, which reflected great credit on BR for its organisation and foresight. Although barely remembered and apparently unrecorded by any photographer, '55XXs' once worked empty stock between Paddington and Old Oak Common around 1929–30. It was nice to see the beautifully repainted Hymek on the move, even if not yet under her own power, returning to a depot from which it once regularly worked.

The recently announced new BR policy on steam railtours suggests that there will be less steam on the main line in future — but then we remember the many reasons trotted out for refusing to run steam in and out of Marylebone. Suddenly the wine and dine steam specials appeared and have done tremendous business ever since. So we shall see. The GWS has not yet participated in these excursions, but whatever happens, the Society's presence out on the main line is certain to continue in one form or another.

CHAPTER 7

THE GWS SMALL RELICS MUSEUM

Fred Gray

THE steam locomotive, in all its gleaming glory will always be the centrepiece of railway preservation in this country, for its attraction and appeal to both enthusiasts and members of the general public is undeniable.

This is perfectly understandable, but any enterprise such as the Great Western Society, seeking to create a comprehensive and wide-ranging display dedicated to the ways and traditions of the Great Western Railway must look beyond the locomotives, as important as they are. Thus, the GWS pays detailed attention to rolling stock and goods wagons in order to show other aspects of the Swindon approach. Nevertheless, the process must not stop there and if we are to provide as complete a picture of GWR activities as we can, we must also deal with the smaller aspects of everyday life on the GWR.

Quite apart from anything else, in an age when we are surrounded by video screens, microchips and computers, people take great pleasure in browsing over the 'bits and pieces' of a fondly-remembered bygone age. In addition to the important role of presenting a complete picture and not just concentrating on locomotives to the exclusion of all else, the preservation and display of smaller items helps to set the engines and carriages in context and brings the whole memory of the GWR to life in a unique fashion.

A quarter of a century ago, the Great Western Society was founded because it was seen by a few that a highly-regarded page in our industrial history was about to be turned and that the artefacts of that history would probably be lost for ever. The preservation of locomotives and rolling stock then proceeded apace for the next 15 years. Of course not everyone can own a locomotive and many personal collections of smaller

Below: There's far more to railway preservation than trains, as this marvellous display in the Didcot Small Relics Museum illustrates. Everything in this office scene, from chair to inkpots, carries the GWR inscription. *Michael Callard.*

Left: Gas lamps, once common throughout Britain were scrapped in their thousands and are now much sought after by private railways. The Museum houses a large number of such characteristic relics. *Michael Callard.*

items were assembled: tickets, travel books, jig-saw puzzles, posters, official documents, cutlery, china, furniture, uniforms, oil lamps and perhaps with some assistance from a rich aunt or a more than understanding bank manager, a nameplate or two!

The list is inexhaustible almost, and a decade or so ago a handful of GWS members interested in this aspect of preservation also turned their attentions to station buildings and platform equipment, lamp standards, fencing, huts and signalling. Gradually a collection accumulated, some of it stored at Didcot, some items stored in members' attics and garages. However, what was sometimes thought at the time, and in some quarters persists to the present day, is the idea that rescuing a given item from the scrapman is the end of story. It is, on the other hand, just the beginning. It's no use transferring a crumbling piece of railway history from one dump to another. It will still be lost unless it receives care and attention and is stored in a protective environment. It became clear to us that we should care for the items which had already been acquired, rather than indulge in continuing relentless preservation for its own sake, and that an organisation was necessary to tackle the backlog of items needing urgent attention. Secondly, suitable storage and display facilities were needed: thus was born the germ of an idea for the GWS Small Relics Museum, at Didcot.

The journey to this goal was long and arduous. As in all preservation matters, nothing much could be done without money. To earn that money you need people coming through the gate, attracted by the spectacle of working steam engines and a catering establishment, both of which had to have financial priority. In the meantime we had literally hundreds and hundreds of items needing restoration for which time and money were given directly by the members involved, a process which continues today, with further welcome assistance from the Great Western Trust. Members still need to have the time to devote to restoration jobs however, and this can sometimes be more difficult to find than finance!

As the collection began to look more presentable, it was possible on certain Gala Days to mount exhibitions in the compartments of the vintage coaches. The popularity of these displays was never in doubt, judging by the long queues waiting to come in and the coins dropped in a carefully placed fire-bucket near the exit! There were problems however: the setting up and subsequent dismantling of the display was time-consuming and tiring, and stewarding the valuable items also required sleeping in the coach overnight, at weekend events.

This was inconvenient and far from ideal for many different reasons.

This did not go unnoticed in the Society and the GWS Council eventually sanctioned construction of a building for a small relics display, after which a foundation stone was ceremonially laid by the Hon. W.H. McAlpine on October 10 1981. A Manpower Services Commission scheme assisted in the construction of the building.

Seven months later the new building was handed over to the Curator and his museum team for fitting-out. From our own resources and with our own labour an electrical installation was provided, whilst a member gave us a false ceiling, for which we were grateful, while our Antiquary Group provided the cash needed to construct showcases. Steel roller-shutters were fitted to all doors and windows.

In the meantime our other responsibilities on the Didcot branch line needed constant attention. The restoration of a 'pagoda' waiting-shelter was just as important as any other item in need of attention and the display in what we term 'the garden' was also in our care.

August 29 1982 was a typically English summer's day, and it marked the end of one struggle and the beginning of another. The Museum Curator and Mrs Sheila Prior, widow of one former long-serving railwayman John Prior, together with some of his ex-colleagues, unveiled a GWR platform seat dedicated to the memory of friends who made the ultimate sacrifice in World War II. Then BBC television personality John Craven performed the time-

One of the many signs and notices displayed in the Small Relics Museum and cared for by the Great Western Trust. *Michael Callard.*

Right: A selection of GWR books and pamphlets, displayed in the Museum in an authentic Company rack. These publications were as much a part of the Swindon tradition as copper and brass.

Far right: A display devoted to the GWR's prestige 'Cheltenham Flyer,' the fastest train in the world in the early 1930s.
Both: Michael Callard.

honoured ribbon-cutting ceremony to declare the Small Relics Museum open.

We are currently embarking on our fourth season, which is also our Society's Silver Jubilee, and we can look back on the last three years with immense satisfaction. The success of the Museum is beyond doubt and in some respects this success has become a two-edged sword. If for some reason (usually staff shortages) we cannot open the Museum, the 'disgusted' visitor from wherever heaps his wrath on our heads, either verbally or on paper. We do try and ensure that the Museum is open as frequently as possible, but there are problems occasionally.

With the formation of the Great Western Trust to protect all the items in our care, our reputation as a seriously-founded and well-run museum now goes before us, with organisations such as British Rail, Madame Tussauds, the GWR Royal Hotel, Paddington and the BBC coming to us for guidance on various matters. Where possible we help out and sometimes provide tuition to 'O' and 'A' level students, or University students undertaking research. To add icing to the cake we learned in December 1985 that we had won an award in the Association of Railway Preservation Societies Best Preserved Station Competition for Didcot Halt and the wonderful Radstock signal box, for which our Bristol Group members take their part in sharing this accolade.

The members of the museum group perform many normally 'unseen' duties of the railway preservation movement. We steward the museum from March to October each year, care for the exhibits and maintain the building. We keep a constant wary eye on how the market is operating at sales and exhibitions, prepare inventories and answer the many letters we get from inquiring enthusiasts or members of the public. We are all volunteers and without the continual support of the enthusiastic museum team our efforts would founder. Restoration is a relentless task and our volunteers do a good job. I try to spend some time each evening on this work, in addition to annual holidays, and even Christmas with the target of fully restoring at least one item per week, on average. This rate of output has now been religiously adhered to non-stop for 11 years, with breaks from this routine dictated only by the events calendar at Didcot such as work-weeks, schools steamings, and last year GWS 150, which cost the progress of 16 evenings work. Fortunately, this has been made-up since to produce the 'one item a week' average required and it is now possible to restore items as soon as they arrive — we have beaten the backlog — but we have an ever increasing maintenance problem in its place.

Having now established our museum, which we believe to be unique in the preservation movement, we now need to look to the future. In order to maintain our reputation as the foremost GWR authority it is necessary to have ready access to the vast amount of information we now hold, and to that end a library building is needed with an adequate computer-controlled indexing system. We estimate that we now have in excess of 30,000 items and it needs little imagination to realise how time-consuming the process of search can be without some sort of mechanical assistance. It is also our aim in the future to provide facilities for parents who by necessity have to bring children to Didcot who are too young to appreciate the museum. This will take the form of a gauge 'O' working electric model railway comprised entirely of tinplate products from such revered manufacturers as Frank Hornby, of Binns Road Liverpool, Bassett-Lowke of Northampton, Bing and any other equipment that takes our fancy. We think this will be very popular indeed.

Once again, money will be needed to turn these dreams into reality, but that's what railway preservation is all about, and we've come a long way since 1961! In the year 2011, the GWS will be celebrating its Golden Jubilee, and while it is unlikely that I shall be at Didcot to see it, I hope I'll be able to watch from my 'booking office in the sky' and see that future generations will still be able to admire the high quality standards established by the Great Western Railway.

Below: The last word in small relics . . .

CHAPTER 8
GWR STEAM AT WORK

Of the four pre Nationalisation railway companies of Great Britain, the Great Western Railway was the one Company which retained most of its individuality and charisma. Its cabside brass numberplates remained unchanged and the splendid lined Brunswick green livery survived unscathed. It was this proud individuality which inspired the formation of the GWS in 1961, and this final chapter presents a last reminder of GWR steam at work, depicting some of Didcot's preserved engines of today, in everyday service prior to preservation.

Above: 'Prairie' tank No. 5572 ambles past Plymouth Laira with the Plymouth-Tavistock 'push-pull' of August 30 1961.

Left: No. 5900 *Hinderton Hall* passes Brewham on July 2 1955, with the 8am Birmingham-Weymouth service.
Both: R. C. Riley.

Right: No. 7808 *Cookham Manor* stands in the sun at Swindon shed on September 21 1964, flanked by 'Hymek' diesel-hydraulic No. D 7087 and Riddles '9F' 2–10–0 No. 92203, which is now named *Black Prince* and preserved on the East Somerset Railway. No. 7808 was completed at Swindon in March 1938 using the wheels and motion from withdrawn 'Mogul' No. 4369, of Weymouth shed. Quite where the GWR got No. 7808's name from is a matter of conjecture, as there is no record of a Cookham Manor ever having existed, at least in the 20th century! *Brian Stephenson.*

Below: *Cookham Manor* pilots 'King' 4–6–0 No. 6002 *King William IV*, hauling the down 'Royal Duchy' — the 1.30pm Paddington-Penzance — of August 8 1959. The train is climbing Dainton Bank. *Hugh Ballantyne.*

Right: 2–6–2T No. 6106, completed at Swindon in May 1931 at a cost of £4,160 (including £847 for the boiler!), stands at Brimscombe shed, in the Stroud 'Golden Valley,' on September 26 1964. The engine was one of a class of 70 new large 'Prairies' introduced in the early 1930s to speed up the London suburban services previously handled by the 'County' tanks. Except for the two running lines, this very attractive scene has been swept away. Brimscombe's small sub-shed (to Gloucester) housed the Sapperton banking engine, on which duty No. 6106 was engaged. *Hugh Ballantyne.*

Above: '56XX' 0–6–2T No. 6697 takes the sinuous route through Hockley with a Stephenson Locomotive Society Birmingham Snow Hill-Chester special, March 27 1966. *Brian Stephenson*.

Left: Collett 'Castle' 4–6–0 No. 5051, then named *Earl Bathurst*, stands at Old Oak Common, awaiting its next duty, on September 30 1958. *R.C. Riley*.

Below: The splendour of Swindon: 'Modified Hall' No. 6998 *Burton Agnes Hall* stands in immaculate ex-works condition at Swindon on August 22 1961. The engine was completed on January 28 1949 at a cost of £8,529, plus £2,035 for its tender. No. 6998 had run 554,089 miles by December 1963 and was withdrawn on January 3 1966. *Brian Stephenson*.

Top: Classic GWR steam at work in a classic GWR location. 'Modified Hall' 4–6–0 No. 6998 *Burton Agnes Hall* hurries through Sonning Cutting, heading for London, shortly after lunch on April 19 1954. *R.J. Blenkinsop*

Above: on May 31 1963 'Castle' 4–6–0 No. 5029 *Nunney Castle* stands at the down platform at Bath, with the 4.33pm Salisbury-Bristol Temple Meads Service. Note the GWR water column and the curious signalbox, perched atop the canopy. *Nunney Castle* is yet to be restored to working order at Didcot, from scrapyard condition — part of the Society's continuing task. *Hugh Ballantyne.*

Right: 2–8–2T No. 7202 stands at Salisbury on September 2 1952. This locomotive also has yet to be restored to working order at Didcot — the voluntary help of new GWS members in projects like this will be very welcome! *Colid Caddy.*